الانتفاضة

intifada

by Joshua Seraphim

𝕷

Leilah Publications

Intifada
Copyright © 2011 Joshua Seraphim Leilah Publications
All rights reserved.

To order wholesale, please contact:
American Wholesale Book Company (205) 956-4151
Ingram Book Company (800) 937-8000
Baker & Taylor (800) 775-1100

Leilah Publications
P.O. Box 1863 Tempe, AZ 85280 U.S.A.

Leilah Publications is an underground publishing company producing & investing in cutting edge, avante-garde artists, writers, musicians, and entertainers. We publish unconventional media that breaks all conceptual boundaries between the mystical..macabre..and the erotic. Our artistic material explores the boundaries of human consciousness, psychology, and sexuality by using literature, poetry, music, art, the occult, and theatre. Leilah Publications is a publishing company for the 21st century, not the 20th.

1

"Hitherto shalt thou come, but no further: and here shall thy proud waves be stayed."

- Job 38:11.

Contents

"...the Generals of the Stones are ready."
- Palestinian

Preface

It is the obligation of persons with decent and moral character during times of repression, thuggery, psychological terrorism, and disinformation to revolt against malevolent institutions, movements, and programs asserting themselves vehicles of enlightenment and progress in the human condition. Spiritual and social institutions that assert their programs as exemplary modules of spiritual advancement must be held accountable by counsel of their peers, and if proven virulent and malevolent, failing in their original statues; abolished.

Prodigious minds contributed throughout the centuries to the pillars of art, classics, literature, music, spiritual fraternity, and the sciences; they are the custodians of the Invisible College, a Cabal of erotic enlightenment and artistic understanding of the darkest depths of the human condition. These prodigies are found in many Christian, Muslim, and other fraternal societies that function exclusively from the occult bullshit that permeates the Internet today. The *Knights of Malta, Ancient and Accepted Scottish Rite of Freemasonry, Order of the Eastern Star, York Rite of Freemasonry, Ordine Militare e Religioso dei Cavalieri di Cristo, Benevolent and Protective Order of Elks, Nizāriyyah* or *Nizārī Ismā'īlīs*, the *Qadiria Boutshishia, Naqshbandi*, the *Chishti*, the *Nimatullahi*, the *Qadiriyyah*, the *Qalandariyya*, the *Sarwari Qadiri*, the *Shadhliyya* and the *Suhrawardiyya* Sufi Orders - all are the cultural pillars of prodigy in art, science, theology, music, and literature.

3

Fraternal organizations that **contribute service and endowment** to humanity, that hold the family as sacred; these are the true pillars of the **Intifada** against virulent "magical orders" operating now as modules of commercialism and juvenile entitlement. These contemporary "magical orders" are infectious to logic and reason; they are only products, easily marketable in a self-published digital world that knows little distinction between research and ranting. Satanic "synagogues" and "churches," like the *"Church of Satan," "Order of Nine Angels," "First Church of Satan," "Synagogue of Satan,"* Scientology, American "Guru" movements such as *"Sathya Sai Baba,"* Osho movement and "Osho Foundation," Shambhala Buddhism, particularly Thelema and Thelemic 'organizations;' *"Ordo Templi Orientis,*®" *"Holy Order of Ra-Hoor-Khuit," "Illuminati Order Societas O.T.O.," "Thelemic Golden Dawn," "Open Source Order of the Golden Dawn," "Antiquities of the Illuminati,"* and various Thelemic groups too spurious to list are nothing more than extensions of personal delusion and fantasies of entitlement.

History is beginning one revolution at a time building to a crucible of human excess and depravity. *Intifada* in Arabic translates as "uprising,' or "revolt." An 'Intifada,' is obligated to occur against occult organizations that have become merely a shell of shells in the Invisible College, spurning initiations laced with lineage disputes, and internecine group melodrama. Modern occult groups and their personalities have grown more absorbed in presentation, especially on the Internet, ignoring magical content and development of personal power. Rituals and degrees have lost their mystique and relevance when readily available on the Internet at the click of fingers, rather than a physical journey to a lodge, library, workshop, or university. No longer is there such a thing as "occult."

It is no less the goal of our affiliates, colleagues, researchers, prodigious artists, initiated Brethren and Matrons, confederates to revolt against, expose, and abolish the afore-listed "magical orders." When in good faith, persons of honorable character strive to better existing social institutions, to act in accords of enlightenment and fraternity furthering the human condition in synchronicities of science, religion, and technology; it is the obligation of these honorable societies to revolt against and abolish virulent and malevolent collusions, namely the afore-listed " magical associations." **Intifada** must be philosophically violent, opposed to the afore-listed "magical-spiritual associations." Revolt must be personal, financial, and social; the movement must be a rebellion against fraud; against slander and libel; against personal delusions of entitlement. Revolt must never cease until the afore-listed contagions are amputated from relevant social strata.

Cabals of enlightenment remain a considerable culture hidden behind developments and prodigious minds in art, music, literature, theatre, and erotica. The Cabal has charted new courses in the arts and remained secret under various collusions, never appearing under the same name; always under a different name or occupation, uncovering new modes of sexual expression and erotica within world religions, their scriptures, and ideologies. They already have revolutionized culture, leading new approaches to technology and social development; pioneering explorations in psychology and technology that will synthesize information with matter. The 'Cabal' known by its many monikers are the pillars of social progress; there influence in social strata is not linear; it is recursive and exponential. Their new social strata will replace obsolete social strata.

The existence of the 'Cabal' is a revolt against global disorder, oppression, and ignorance. The afore-listed "magical organizations" or projects, are the embodiment of social degeneration and maladaptive behavior. Intifada must break down reality tunneling of the past; spiritual fraternity is becoming replaced by Media Mystery Schools. Too much information has been released. Naturally, insurrectionists will counter with an influx of disinformation before we leave. The "Cabal" in the global age has moved from hierarchies to networks. Global and economic managing now comes through networks rather than through hierarchies. Governments network for the same reason non-government organizations, financial agencies, and criminals network: information brokerage.

The notion of an occult Intifada against the listed "magical orders" and projects belongs to a three-dimensional view of history: this view does not regard as essential, superficial dimensions of time and space (which include causes, facts, and visible leaders). It rather emphasizes the dimension of depth, or the 'subterranean' dimension in which forces and influences often act in a decisive manner, and which, more often not than not, cannot be reduced to what is merely human, whether at an individual or a collective level. Intifada is our collective story, our common obligation.

Newer generations are working in our universities, through social media, and entrepreneurial global networks to enact revolutionary changes in social strata and technology that will rupture the fabric of human emotion and artistic expression. New forms of paramedia will enable newer generations to merge artificial intelligence and the human organism, through nanotechnology human emotions and bioart can stretch the levels of consciousness. Newer generations of social entrepreneurs already are changing modules of human intimacy, reaching a new level of human techno-divinity.

These listed "magical orders" and "movements" are infectious to logic and reason; they are only products, easily marketable in a self-published digital world that knows little distinction between research and ranting. Satanic "synagogues" and "churches," like the *"Church of Satan," "Order of Nine Angels," "First Church of Satan," "Synagogue of Satan,"* Scientology, American "Guru" movements such as *"Sathya Sai Baba,"* Osho movement and "Osho Foundation," Shambhala Buddhism, particularly Thelema and Thelemic 'organizations;' *"Ordo Templi Orientis,*®*" "Holy Order of Ra-Hoor-Khuit," "Illuminati Order Societas O.T.O.," "Thelemic Golden Dawn,"*

"*Open Source Order of the Golden Dawn*," "*Antiquities of the Illuminati*," and various Thelemic groups are simply extensions of personal delusion and fantasies of entitlement. Revolt must amputate these contagions from social and human progress in the 21st century.

Uprising

Intifada: *Arabic; 'shaking off,' 'uprising.', an insurrection. a revolt.*

The teachings of the Elite and Elect diffuse throughout our history from secret societies, traced in pedigree and language with esoteric syncretism. In the Twenty-first century, Christianity, Judaism, and Islam all precariously share a fragile world stage, leading societies teasingly close to economic and social ruin in the name of faith and "liberty and equality," the opiate of religions. Consider Esoterica and occult institutions of Freemasonry and appendent bodies, Opus Dei, Hospitaller Order of Malta, and Rosy Cross fraternities that are tagged as conspiratorial "Illuminati" groups, determined to establish a "new world order" fantasized over by conspiracy racketeers. The mystic fraternities I listed, an many unlisted, mindful of their own affairs, engage in acts of charity, education, scholarship, chivalry, and public service for a greater good ignored by a cadre of racketeers in the likes of Alex Jones a seething spokesperson for the producerist fear racket that stains good men and women of these mystic organizations.

Conspiracy personalities David Icke, Alex Jones, Leo Zagami, Rense, and Marrs are uneducated and asinine in appointing Freemasonry and Rosy Cross fraternities at the forefront of conspiracies and plots to enable a "new world order" placing you and me under a sort of fascist neo-satanic global government. Jones, Icke, and other asinine personalities repeatedly cite the elite men and women in our Heritage Roll-Calls as evil characters in a global theatre-like game to abolish civil liberties.

Icke in his book, *The Biggest Secret*, raves over alleged Rosicrucian plots: *"The term Rosi-Crucis was also the origin, quite obviously, of the Rosicrucians, an ancient secret society which has schemed and manipulated to ensure the reptilian bloodlines continue to occupy the positions of power."* {Icke, David. *The Biggest Secret*. Scottsdale, AZ: Bridge of Love Publications, 1999. Pg.143 Print} Icke reveals his clear absurdity over equating Rosicrucians as reptilian overlords: *"They are variously known as the Secret Chiefs, the Hidden Masters, or the Great White Brotherhood and some researchers believe they are the force behind the creation of the Freemasons, Sufis, Knights Templar, Rosicrucians, Theosophical Society, and the Hermetic Order of the Golden Dawn. I think these people are reptilians, some of them anyway."* {Ibid, 245}

Conspiracy producerists, like Icke and Alex Jones unforgivably, and I suspect intentionally, confuse the historic nature of Rosicrucianism and Freemasonry. From Icke, we have this unforgivable rant speaking of King James and the Rosy Cross influence in Biblical translation: *"James knighted Francis Bacon and appointed him too many important positions, including Lord Chancellor of England. Under James's patronage, the Templars, Rosicrucians and other secret societies joined forces under one name, Freemasonry."* {Ibid, 181} He later accuses Rosicrucians of being mind-controlling killers: "The Rosicrucians expanded the use of mind-altering drugs and the Assassins possibly got their very name from the way they employed drugs to mind control their killers." {Ibid, 294}

Alex Jones in his rants on Freemasonry is even more malicious and intentionally derogatory: *"Number one, your father is a 'porch Mason.' They're outside the house. There are three-hundred and sixty degrees of Freemasonry. Your father doesn't even know about those three-sixty. Your father only thinks there's thirty-three."* {Alex Jones Weekly Report Filmed Live November 9th, 2004} Profuse amounts of disinformation and intentionally disingenuous writings are readily available on the Internet to unsuspecting researchers. We can only surmise that the reasons for the conspiracy movement's various cliques diseducation campaign is to line their own coffers, commercializing fear and apprehension in times of social and economic disorientation.

The men and women of our roll calls are prodigies having charted a new expanse across the mind, body, and soul to the farthest reaches of consciousness and space-time continuum. They are part of an elect and elite heritage with pedigreed secrets and an unbroken current of antiquarian initiation. Such pedigreed lines of mystic fraternities synchronized in the early advent of Christian mysteries, adopted throughout generations with esoteric traditions in Arabia.

***Illuminati are indispensable* to human brain engineering, genetics, arts, social strata, and technological advancement.** It is the arcane traditions of the Xristos, synchronized from Egyptian theology and Hermeticism that enable the twin pillars of art and science in the Western Mystery Traditions. Illuminati are indispensable, *but modern occult organizations and their spurious personalities are not.*

Intifada in Arabic translates as "uprising,' or "revolt." An 'Intifada,' is obligated to occur against occult organizations that have become merely a shell of shells in the Invisible College, spurning initiations laced with lineage disputes, and internecine group melodrama. Modern occult groups and their personalities have grown more absorbed in presentation, especially on the Internet, ignoring magical content and development of personal power. Rituals and degrees have lost their mystique and relevance when readily available on the

Internet at the click of fingers, rather than a physical journey to a lodge, library, workshop, or university. No longer is there such a thing as "occult."

One of the major differences between individuals who pursue and study the fine arts, classics, and common individuals in the human condition is the ability to experience the entire spectrum of existence, to adapt and change their environment according to their desire. Occultism often attracts narcissistic personalities who have a grandiose sense of self-value, and they consistently overestimate and overvalue their endowments. They exaggerate their accomplishments and are boastful, arrogant, and pretentious. Many have real talents and abilities, most are simply legends in their own mind tending not to test themselves in the natural echelons.

Their identities are codependent on their emotions, expending critical amounts of energy guarding against feelings of shame, humiliation and protecting them from criticism. It is not uncommon for them to be easily wounded and oscillate between guarding feelings of superiority, against having anyone finding out how inferior they feel compared to their delusions of superiority. Occult personalities, such as Crowley and his Thelemic cult, Golden Dawn personalities Griffin, Zink, and Cherubim are very status oriented and prefer to be with admirers or others who can maintain and inflate their feelings of artificial prodigy.

These megalomaniacs have a strong sense of entitlement, often denied them in professional, social, and academic environments preferring to focus their feelings on lacking qualities. They incapable of taking responsibility for their behavior while ignoring ensuing consequences and prefer to blame others for their moral and professional failures. Their poise is artificial, as they expend maximum efforts in denying, hiding, and lying about their moral failure. Their relationships are frequently superficial. People are regarded either as a danger to their artificially superior status, or as a booster,

11

enabling approval or serving as an audience. While they may be very good at showing concern for others, especially within a group setting, it is a sham. They lack real compassion and emotional depth, too preoccupied with their grandiose fantasies, keeping themselves from feelings of despair, sadness, and emptiness. As a rule their relationship are short and artificial.

They do not see the world clearly; because they are blinded by feelings of entitlement, and delusions of grandeur. They remain unaware of their neuroses, unaware their minds are lost in delusion. Individuals like Griffin, Breeze, and Cherubim who are in positions of artificial "influence" are quickly wounded, often silently, at the slightest perceived insult. Such perceptions descend into paranoia, and feelings of depression, aggression, and recrimination. My experiences in observance of several occult personalities like Griffin, Breeze, Cherubim, and Thelemites indicates that if these individuals do not resolve issues of entitlement they are physically unhealthy, unattractive, and unintelligent, unable to apply intelligence professionally and artistically.

Their strategies for coping moral and artistic failure is to increase their level of controlling behavior. Some become eccentric and withdraw from life into esoteric pursuits, joining occult orders and working their way up artificial magical rankings where they can verify that they are chosen, unique, and special. Some even provoke intense persecution and crucifixion of sorts to prove their grandiose neuroses. They have extreme difficulty in accepting the proposition that nature is arbitrary, capricious, and beautifully chaotic. It is difficult for them to accept themselves and life without a story of grandeur and entitlement. Hence, they attract themselves to grandiose spiritual titles or characters, such as "Grand Master," "Founder," or even "Antichrist."

Thelema is an occult philosophy centred on neo-Gnosticism, Witchcraft, hedonism, and Nietzschian will-based philosophies popularized by Edward Alexander Crowley

{Aleister Crowley} around the year A.D. 1904. Copious cultish organizations have sprouted and multiplied during and after Crowley's lifetime, many of them in their own machinations professing some version of Crowley's teachings. If we exclude the deformed sense of reality that so often bleeds from questionable characters associated with the "Occult," Crowley's teachings and literature were in essence a plagiarism of Christian Gnosticism mixed with ceremonial magic, the hyper-Cynicism of Diogenes of Siope, Nietzsche's will-based philosophies and the hedonism of Francois Rabelais and Marquis D.A.F. de Sade.

All cults stem from a fundamentalism root often from within an established religious tradition. Cults can exploit and abuse members psychologically conditioning the new proselytes into a deformed sense of reality and ideologies. Cults with elaborate and often emotional means of indoctrination often manipulate and wage authoritarian mind control over members. Cults, such as Crowley's "Thelema" are communal totalistic in their organization. Individuals join because of what the group does for them - namely, fulfill and exploit unconscious psychological needs.

The human inclination for spirituality and its latency in the human genome is subject matter than I researched for years in and out of academia. The occult sciences can open one to supernatural and neurological energies, and resources unavailable to the majority of our species for nearly two-thousand years. Permanent neurological and psychological damage can easily result from engaging occult sciences, to dilettantes and the most seasoned occultists. I have personally observed occultists develop severe neuroses and psychotic complexes, and further aggravate pre-existing psychoses, by engaging in energies they could not understand nor took the time and effort to research the "dark arts."

Priests advised and assisted my personal research in University and Church libraries. In the late 1990s, a German woman (Frau) who worked as a hospice nurse advised my esoteric studies and training personally. She was an initiate of an ancient esoteric fraternity active since the seventeenth century later involved with, and supported by the German National Socialist Worker's Party {Nazi}. My teacher, in her mid-50s then, gave me two initiations before I completed my physical and esoteric training with her; a tantric initiation, and a mystical Christian-oriented initiation under Rosicrucian lineage. She directed me to the Rosicrucian societies, and Golden Dawn traditions in Arizona. In Arizona, I began a series of Golden Dawn initiations in 1999 that culminated with an initiation into the Lover's Triad inside the Great Pyramid of Giza, in Egypt, 2004, and the beginning of my practicing the mind and body shaping techniques of Dr. Christopher S. Hyatt. Dr. Hyatt advised my esoteric and professional pursuits from 2005-2007.

Collusion

Our souls, it is thought by the ancient Egyptians, ascended from the netherworlds. We are a race with a greater heritage guided by the stars, monuments, and imperial religions. According to many ancient creation myths, Mankind fell in a great exodus from the stars; swarms of souls emerged from the Firmament, yet not every man and woman is not from the light. In the nexus between the stars and space, the All-Seeing Eye ever-peers over this primeval exodus, which occurred before the Sun and Moon were created. Illuminati unlock the secrets of death and life, and oversee the evolution of the species towards a manifest destiny.

Every man and women whose blood retains the secrets of this hidden Heritage *knows* there has existed already an *Invisible College*, a Cabal that is our collective past, united in the bonds of brotherhood and in perfect beauty, ordained to act as an exterior *collegium regium* in order to preserve and safeguard the Lost Mysteries of Antiquity. These invisible fraternities have had many epithets and by each name has each secret fraternity been covered by another: Fraternity of the Rose Cross, Knights Templar, Bavarian Illuminati, Freemasons, Order of Malta, Order of the Eastern Star, Order of the Dragon, Ecclesia Gnostica, Golden Dawn, and other organizations keeping silence. Fratres and Sorores, Brethren and Matrons of these elect and secret fraternities are

Potentates of the Serpent, Illuminates of the Ancient Mysteries and Kindred Sciences, Inheritors of a Dying World whom are dedicated in silence to extend, to preserve the bloodlines of Eve and Lilith – the ancient initiators of Man in the Nightside of Eden.

In all the elegant cities of the ancient world, there were temples for public worship and offering. In every hamlet also were philosophers and mystics, deeply versed in Nature's secrets. These individuals banded together, forming reclusive, sheltered philosophic and religious academies. The elite and initiated of these groups were known as the *Invisible College*. Many of the great minds of antiquity were initiated into these secret fraternities by shadowed rites, some of which were extremely cruel and sadistic.

Alexander Wilder defines the Mysteries as *"Sacred dramas performed at stated periods. The most celebrated were those of Isis, Sabazius, Cybele, and Eleusis."* After being received in the Lodges and subterranean Temples, the initiates were instructed in the secret wisdom that had been preserved for ages. Oaths were taken under the penalties of death and indescribable torture for the postulant and his family…if he should break them. Plato, an initiate of one of these sacred orders, was severely punished by his own Academy because in his tracts he revealed to the public many of the secret philosophic principles of the Eleusian rites.

The Great Pagan nations of Rome, Athens, Carthage, Babylonian, Canaan, and Egypt dictated not only an Imperial religion, but secret academies into which the Epopts alone have gained entry. Many of these academies from Ephesus to Alexandria vanished from history without revealing their secrets. Few have survived the test of æons and their mysterious alphabets and ciphers are still preserved by Initiates avowed to silence. The elaborate ritualism of Freemasonry and its higher degrees in the *York Rite, Ancient & Accepted Scottish Rite, Ancient and Primitive Rite of*

Memphis-Misraïm is based on the trials to which candidates were subjected by the ancient hierophants to judge their merit and religious stature.

Shortly before the Christian era, half-faith began to lead the world to ruin, faith bred a divorce from reason a psychic schizophrenia of Man's spirit and will. A great revival of the mystery traditions occur every age when the world is in need of refuge from the poisonous religions of superstition and greed. That the secrets of the Orient, the mysteries of Serapis, Mani, and Meithras, influenced the early Church fathers is evident in the early canons of Christian writers. Imperial edicts were powerless to stay this pre-Christian revival of the mystery traditions. As the Roman Imperium adopted as its civil religion the teachings of the Nazarene reformed with Pauline and Petrine canon, the mystery traditions grew audacious and exclusive from a once pagan Rome, at the same time were the mysteries humble and open. It is at the point of the ruinous Medieval Ages did the mysteries become confounded as Mysticism and Occultism, mired in the witch-hysteria betwixt each.

The arts and sciences of the Magi were concealed under the shadows of Thebes, Memphis, and Ephesus; though imperfectly held in trust by Gnosticism, the Ancient Mysteries remain well preserved in Rosicruciana and Freemasonry. Religious orders such as the Rosicrucians, Freemasonry {York, Scot, and Memphis-Misraïm Rites}, Theosophical Society, Knights Templar, Bavarian Order of Perfectibilists {later, Illuminated Seers of Bavaria, or simply, Bavarian Illuminati}, Golden Dawn, Order of the Assassins, Roshaniyya, Cathari, Knights Hospitaller of Malta, all exist or existed in history as custodians of secret knowledge.

Such ordained knowledge transmitted by secret societies can be traced through rituals, and language with religious syncretism. From the twenty-first century to the time when Mankind first recorded myths about the stars and the gods, Egypt has been the repository of imperial magic and religion. The Magi of ancient Egypt knew that a manifest destiny existed, and was necessary for a greater heritage of the race. For thousands of years this heritage and manifest destiny has been safeguarded through the rise and fall of world empires, world wars, and the advent of religions. Across the Æons we have sought to emulate the gods and stars above, hereupon earth and inside our own immortal souls.

Hidden and masked, there exists unknown to the great nations, a very secret Order of Epopts, whose object is the reformation of the world, and the preeminent elevation of the elder race by the congregation of good men and women to oppose the progress of the suppression of religious dignity. Secret societies have existed since Mankind first began to record its myths and religions. For thousands of years societies have existed safeguarding secret religious teachings transmitted through the generations. Monuments, Apocrypha, ordained occult knowledge, catacombs, forgotten ciphers, and secret sacrifices all have been kept guarded by the heritage of the Illuminati, an umbrella term for a vast matrix of secret societies. *Illuminati* are at the forefront of many conspiracy theories pertaining to religion and a shadow history.

This ordained knowledge transmitted by secret societies can be traced through rituals, and language with religious syncretism. From the twenty-first century to the time when Mankind first recorded myths about the stars and the gods, Egypt has been the repository of imperial magic and religion. The Adepts who issued the Tarot, Kabbalah, and other arcana knew that a manifest destiny existed, and was necessary for a greater heritage of the species. For thousands of years this heritage and manifest destiny has been safeguarded through the rise and fall of world empires, world wars, and the advent of religions. Across the Æons we have sought to emulate the gods and stars above, hereupon earth

18

and inside our own genome. Mankind does have a manifest destiny; to reach deep into our blood and beyond the stars.

The Cabal's hidden traditions were transmitted through ceremony, initiation, hidden sacrifices, and forgotten tongues. Through a fusion of Isma'ili and Sufi mystic teachings with Gnostic Christianity and Jewish Kabbalists, the Legacy of the Gift coagulated from these three esoteric currents during the era of the Crusades. Egypt is the bygone birthplace of esoteric teachings. We can trace synchronous threads of occult knowledge progressing into Gnostic, Isma'ili, and Kabbalist teachings.

Imperial Egypt is the matrilineal progenitor of esoteric teachings that married into the world religions. It is the depository of the Invisible College that has endured, and written histories of Mankind. The Magi of Egypt initiated an imperial religion based upon antediluvian magic. The marriage of forgotten alphabets with secret funerary rites and secret sacrifices birthed the foundations of magic preserved in papyri, sculpted carvings, mortuary scrolls, frescoes, monolithic temples, painted jewelry, and sarcophagi. These mysteries spawned an esoteric migration from Egypt into the surrounding worlds of ancient Greece, Rome, Persia, and beyond. The Eleusinian teachings believed to have been initiated and practiced as initiation ceremonies for the cults of Demeter and Persephone beginning around 1500^{BC} during the Mycenaean Era.

The Mysteries were based on a legend revolving around Demeter, goddess of agriculture and fertility. According to the myth, Demeter's daughter Persephone was gathering flowers with maidens one day, when she was seen by Hades, god of death and the underworld. Hades fell in love with Persephone and kidnapped her, taking her to his underworld kingdom where the dead lay dreaming. Distraught, Demeter searched high and low for her daughter; in her distress, she neglected her duties of bestowing fertility to mortals. Subsequently, this caused a terrible draught in which families suffered and children starved. (Although the dry season is summer in Greece, this catastrophe is often associated with winter.)

During her search, Demeter wandered ever peering into the netherworlds, having many minor escapades along the way, including one in which she teaches the secrets of agriculture to *Triptolemus*. Finally, by consulting Zeus, Demeter reunites with her daughter Persephone and the earth returns to its former prosperity: the first spring. Persephone was unable to remain in the land of life; while in the underworld she had eaten six seeds of a pomegranate that Hades had given her, thus magically she was bound to the netherworlds for six months of the year (Autumn & Winter) but was allowed by Zeus and Hades to stay on the earth for the remaining six months (Spring & Summer).

The Eleusinian mysteries celebrated Persephone's return, for it was also the return of plants and of agrarian harvest to the earth. Persephone had gone into the underworld (beneath the earth, like seeds in the winter), then returned to the land of life: her rebirth is symbolic of the rebirth of all agriculture during the spring and, by extension, all life on earth. The Eleusinian rites were held every five years for about two millennia. In the Homeric Hymn to Demeter, a "King Celeus" is heard to have been one of the first men to learn the secret rites and mysteries of her cult, as well as one of the original priests, along with *Diocles*, *Eumolpos*, *Polyxeinus*, and *Triptolemus*, Celeus' son, who had supposedly learned agriculture from Demeter.

Under *Pisistratus* of Athens, the Eleusinian Mysteries became pan-Hellenic and pilgrims from all over the ancient world immigrated to Greece to attend the ceremonies that lasted nine days. Around 300^{BC}, the state took over control of the Mysteries; they were specifically controlled by two families, the *Eumolpidae* and the *Kerykes*. This led to a vast increase in the number of initiates. The only requirements for membership were a lack of "blood-guilt," meaning having never committed murder, and not being a barbarian Men, women and even slaves were allowed to be initiated.

The Egyptians entertained no doubt about the existence, the persistence, or the firmament of the præter-human spirit or ghosts of man. Taking into account the scrolls and mortuary texts that whisper of Ægyptian secret rituals in the times before the first Pharaohs, the worship of the ghosts or ancestral spirits of the dead was that which followed the two previous dynasties of the elemental powers of earth and the *Kronidae* in Ægyptian astronomical mythology. We know these præter-human intelligences from the genesis of Ægyptian pantheon in nature as elemental powers or animistic spirits, which were deified because they were superhuman, and therefore not human.

Sut, the soul of darkness; Horus, the soul of light; Shu, the soul of air or breathing force; Seb, soul of earth; Nu (or Num), the soul of water; Ra, as soul of the sun, were gods, but these antediluvian beings did not birth from any dead men's ghosts. Moreover, Man did not make his gods in his own image, Ægyptian theology was propagated by Magi who closely observed the laws of nature, astronomical processions, mathematics, architecture, and spiritual phenomena. Such ordained knowledge was preserved in the language of hieroglyphs and hidden alphabets. In the beginning of Ægyptian creationism was the void, otherwise designated the abyss.

Darkness being the primordial unmanifest point, or first cause (called by the Persian Magi, *qutub*), it followed naturally that prototypes in religious representation should be a figure of darkness. This was the mythical dragon, or serpent *Apep*, the ever-devouring reptile, the monster Maw, the prototype of evil in nature. Apep rose up by night from the abyss and coiled about the Mount of Earth as the swallower of the light; who in another phase drank up all the sacred Nile, as the dreaded dragon of southern drought. The voice of this huge, serpent was the thunder that shook the firmament; the drought was its blasting breath that dried up the Nile inundations and withered fertile vegetation. Other præter-human beings of the void were likewise elemental, antinomian to agriculture and Man. These were the spawn of pestilence, drought, and plague.

The aim of initiation into the mysteries is to prepare for immortality. By taking up the Great Work and its sacred studies, the neophyte allied his or her entire consciousness and existence to the divine, that uncreated firmament of *limitless light*. This divine substance was never born, never manifest, and shall never perish in the multiverse of infinite diversities. Initiation is the means of rebirth where men and women are strewn asunder into the endless Sea. This endless Sea is the farthest reaches of human consciousness and imagination. The Path of Initiation arrogates strength & skill of Will. Occult initiation is a dire ordeal of the deathless soul as the "Dark Night of the Soul" in the Chapel Perilous of the Grail legend, or the "Valley of the Shadow of Death" often bewitches the initiate.

The underlying obligation of initiation into the Mysteries was that the Preceptors were consecrated brethren, and matrons, of the *Gift* not "layman of the brute herd." When the naked, bound, and pestilent candidate strips the mind of all psychological deconditioning (to unlearn), has mortified and excited the intolerable ache of the flesh (sensory deprivation), abandoned religious memes (occult science), s/he rises from a mystical death to reclaim the divine spark of Light, the Kingdom within. True and real initiation into the Hidden Light of the Arts and Sciences left an indelible mark on the soul. Such a Gift of the Invisible College was played out during a mystical reenactment and orchestrated pageantry of myth.

Through daunting pageantry of mythic recreations, consecrations by scripture and the elements, psychological deconditioning, and sensory deprivation, terror and pity were forcibly impressed upon the Candidate's fractured mind inducing an intolerable ache of the heart. Catharsis has been the fundamental nature of ritual initiation in all ages and sacred institutions of the Invisible College. The Adepts of this Invisible College today and yesterday knew the forbidden arts and sciences.

The great strength of the antiquities of the Illuminati lay in their concealment, never appearing in any place in one single name, but always shrouded by another name and occupation. Within their university, centres are the forgotten sons and daughters of the Pyramids whose progeny birthed bloodlines in power, prophesized in the well of dreams and, made penitence in the Mercy of the Light. These royal Adepts _knew_ the healing arts in their salons, and in their laboratories. The Brethren of the Lodge taught that the limitless Light of **G**omer, **O**z, **D**abar is within a refuge of souls, within the stars themselves. Initiation transmitted this Gift through flesh, bloodline, and scientific advancements. Through our Heritage of the Illuminati, we are never deprived of that Light.

Man is ever-peering into the pervading Eye, as can be seen in the sculptures of the Greeks and Minoans, the papyri and monolithic pyramids of Egypt, the copulating frescoes in rogue Tibetan monasteries, art of the Vatican vaults and basilicas, Thuggee shrines to Kali in Hindu cremation grounds, in the Kachina tales of the Hopi, in African Obeah rituals, even in the monasteries of the Benedictines.

The Gates of immortality are always open to the initiated sons and daughters of the College; they are the custodians of the gardens, monasteries, bloodlines that have built our society. The infinitude of the All-Seeing Eye is allegorically sexual, elaborated through bloodlines of Epopts and secret societies. Religions invoke faith as an anesthesia in the absence of the sacred. Mankind is the true artist, having created the divine stage of gods, archons, demons, goddesses, and infernal fallen angels as a stellar play, an immemorial story of the soul captured in the Major Arcana of the Tarot.

Faith is a measurement of the divine stage, highlighted in the procession of the Tarot Trumps, created by the human impetus to the Holy. The Adepts who issued the Tarot, and forgotten alphabets of magic, did not refer to the Great Work as *"my"* Will, *"my"* religion, *"my"* Path. Physicist Erwin Rudolf Josef Alexander Schrödinger writes: *"the goal of Man is to preserve his Karma and to develop it further…when man dies his Karma lives and creates for itself another carrier."* Their goal was to become the Way, to form a synergistic bloodline that echoes the secret saturnalia and sacred institutions began by the progenitors of Egypt's Imperial Illuminati.

The Initiate, one whom adopts the Hermit life, and duly invokes the four Hermetic powers of the Sphinx has taken up the holy obligations of rectitude, and sacrifice, thus instead of seeking a refuge of souls, the Initiate of the Mysteries has *become* a refuge of Light. The four Hermetic powers of the Sphinx respectively, are: *scire, velle, audere, tacere*, and the least understood "fifth" power, ire. *"To Know, to Will, to Dare*, to **Keep Silence**, and *to Go."* In their perilous quest for lust, the secret sacrifices, and forgotten rites are kept from those who shun destinies. The grace of destiny is of the elect, for many are called, few chosen.

The illuminated minds of the Mysteries viewed the reformation of the world's religions, and the procession of the stars across and beyond time, between the world of the living and the world of the dead. Illuminati conceal the secrets of G.O.D., the secrets of death and arts of Lust. A brutal ordeal of initiation into the Invisible College is for the Neophyte to be denied the divine Light, thereafter experiencing a common crisis of destiny the Brothers of the Cross refer to as the "Dark Night of the Soul," or as the Templars called it, the *Chapel Perilous.* In this psychological terror, the Rose disintegrates in an alchemical crisis of the human body and mind. If the ordeal is overcome, the Neophyte awakens from the sleep of history and is initiated into a system that will change his physiological & psychological constructs.

The Neophyte who overcomes the ordeal of initiation breaks through barriers of social – political conditioning, moral and religious upbringing to develop prodigies in all levels of society who can maintain nature's critical balance in the romantic history of our species. To this "Invisible College," every wise man and woman has an indefeasible right to belong by the constitutions of his or her dignity and virtue, as each, if even unbeknownst to the other, are divided for love's sake, to unite in fraternity and sorority under the One Light of Truth, the Truth of Darkness, that is the dark Arts, the Science of the Stars, the Keys of Religion, the Veil of the Antediluvian Mysteries.

Those who challenged the burning grounds, the desert sands, and the black earth, know silently that numerous orders, congregations, temples, societies, etc., have been inaugurated during the last one hundred years all following lineages of Occult Art and Science. From the ashrams of Calcutta, India and Vajrayana monasteries of Tibet to the basilicas of Rome, and York Lodges of the Free & Accepted Masons, the Adepts of these sacred institutions consecrated rites and sacrifices where the living and dead prevailed over the destroyers of form, extinguishers of breath, seizers of karmic memory, and eclipsers of æthereal Light. Naïve is the lost soul whom denies the Legacy of the Gift {the Illuminati *inheritance*} was not birthed in Love, beings copulating as Man lay in lust with Angels..one heritage..one *blood.*

The intelligences illuminated by study we will examine in this book include the carnal knowledge of trance-states, physiology, time-induced hallucinogens {used by the ancient Order of Assassins, the Isma'ili *Hashashiyya*}, and introduced the Ægyptian doctrine of spiritual transmigration. The Adepts learned to transmigrate the æthers, enter shamanic states of awareness, and penetrate infinite diversities of space-time. The Invisible College Adepts and their students knew these secret rituals not only as gateways into spiritual paths the orthodox priesthoods considered unnatural, but also for their aesthetic beauty – as revelations of **Art**. *"The Anesthetic Revelation is the Initiation of Man into the Immemorial Mystery of the Open Secret of Being, revealed as the Inevitable Vortex of Continuity."*

What the Sufi Adepti called *Qīyâmat* {judgment} and *Qadar* {fate} were divine states of consciousness that only Neophytes who had attained nine degrees of initiation could enter, a garden without walls, a sect without a church, a lost moment of history that refuses to be forgotten, standing outside time, a reproach or challenge to all religious doctrine, to all the cruelty of the exoteric. An invitation to paradise..a nightside of Eden where the well of Man's midnight revealed unspeakable terror and ecstasy to those who dared deny death. Bloodline after bloodline, centuries of secret histories have preserved the Invisible College.

A synchronicity of initiation from ancient Ægyptian mortuary rites to secret saturnalia of Mithraic temples and ceremonies of the Scottish and York Rites have become the axis of the one true Invisible College. Myths, superstitions, dogmas, creeds, and metaphysical theologies give way to the beginnings of a 'Science of Religions.' This enlightened propensity seems to make room for a sort of 'theistic science' that segregates Occult arts and sciences from philosophic schizophrenia, i.e., the ongoing polemic between "magic," and mysticism. On the uniformity of the secret doctrines, Madame Helena Petrovna Blavatsky writes: *"The best proof you can have of the fact is that every ancient religious, or rather philosophical, cult consisted of an esoteric or secret teaching, and an exoteric (outward public) worship. Furthermore, it is a well-known fact that the MYSTERIES of the ancients comprised with every nation the "greater" (secret) and "Lesser" (public) MYSTERIES -- e.g. in the celebrated solemnities called the Eleusinia, in Greece. From the Hierophants of Samothrace, Egypt, and the initiated Brahmins of the India of old, down to the later Hebrew Rabbis, all preserved, for fear of profanation, their real bona fide beliefs secret. The Jewish Rabbis called their secular religious series the Mercavah (the exterior body), "the vehicle," or, the covering which contains the hidden soul. -- i.e., their highest secret knowledge. Not one of the ancient nations ever imparted through its priests its real philosophical secrets to the masses, but allotted to the latter only the husks. Northern Buddhism has its "greater" and it's "lesser" vehicle, known as the Mahayana, the esoteric, and the Hinayana, the exoteric, Schools. Nor can you blame them for such secrecy; for surely you would not think of feeding your flock of sheep on learned dissertations on botany instead of on grass? Pythagoras called this Gnosis "the knowledge of things that are," or e gnosis ton onton, and preserved that knowledge for his pledged disciples only: for those who could digest such mental food and feel satisfied; and he pledged them to silence and secrecy. Occult alphabets and secret ciphers are the development of the old Egyptian hieratic writings, the secret of which were, in the days of old, in the possession only of the Hierogrammatists, or initiated Egyptian priests. Ammonius Saccas, as his biographers tell us, bound his pupils by oath not to divulge his higher doctrines except to those who had already been instructed in preliminary knowledge, and who were bound by a pledge. Finally, do we not find the same even in early Christianity, among the Gnostics, and even in the teachings of Christ? Did he not speak to the multitudes in parables which had a two-fold meaning, and explain his reasons only to his disciples? "To you," he says, "it is given to know the mysteries of the kingdom of heaven; but unto them that are without, all these things are done in parables" (Mark iv. 11). "The Essenes of Judea and Carmel made similar distinctions, dividing their adherents into neophytes, brethren, and the perfect, or those initiated" (Eclec. Phil.). Examples might be brought from every country to this effect.*

The Arcanum so well-articulated by Madame Blavatsky speaks of spiritual keys {*"occult alphabets and secret ciphers"}* used by Adepts to yield up oracles of time-space and direct language between the wayfaring Hermits and their students to preserve secretly psychotechnology capable of changing the species and unlocking the science of the soul. Every footstep into the unknown, like the mystic path of the Fool in the Tarot Arcana, yielded the fullness of wise-blooded wisdom of the Ages. Such perilous steps into the Temples at Ephesus, Delphi, Alexandria, Alamut and many other sacred sanctuaries induced a denial of the finite self, a sort of ascetic deprivation found in religious experiences to be doorways to a greater life. This final mystery intertwines all Gnostic, Hermetic, and Ægyptian mysteries in all mystical writings past and future.

Love is the elixir where the soul migrates from the endless Void of Nothing, separating betwixt all that is nature and beast, and from the visible world into the immaterial fluid of consciousness...the *soul*. Love, rather agapæ, or Imperial Love, is the highest virtue initiates seek who chose to walk the path laid out in the archaic Tarot decks. Agapæ is the foundation of all initiations, threading together ritual systems explored in present and immemorial secret societies. Initiations possess guides and signposts of progress. Many of the ordeals are rooted in the Tarot Arcana, laid out for Neophytes to navigate.

These ordeals and psychological tribulations clearly relate to intimacy and sexual relationships as the Neophyte almost immediately following the days of his initiation encounters a seductive nymph who tests the levels of commitment, the nature and loyalty of the Neophyte to his, or her, work, and finally their understanding of the physical relationship they presently are engaged or soon will engage in. Another ordeal is a test of loyalty to ones initiating Brotherhood or Preceptor, in effect, the trial does not measure physical loyalty but fidelity to the oaths, and principles set forth in the initiation ceremony. The ordeals of the Adept are of the direst, for they are spiritual ordeals of perfect beauty, of faith and true love. Here, the fool of the Tarot receives the fullness of initiation in the heart.

In such ordeals of psychological, physiological, and spiritual fitness, the soul finds itself with nothing, utterly stripped and naked; it can do nothing because it is stripped of all manner of power sitting in its own infinitude of nothingness. This powerlessness felt by the initiate in his conjuring at once deprives and transcends the senses. The more intimate these experiences are, they grow supersensible to the point of mystic silence imposed upon the senses, as the soul soon feels placed in a vast and profound solitude; this is often symbolized by oceans or deserts in the writings of Illuminati Hermits. Many Adepts soon successfully pass these ordeals and find themselves living in actual desert settings or rural areas. In this abyss of true love and wisdom the soul gestates, awaiting rebirth by drinking from the wellsprings of agapæ. Yogic Adept Swami Vivekananda writes of certain initiatory states:

"That the mind itself has a higher state of existence, beyond reason, a superconscious state, and that when the mind gets to that higher state, then this knowledge beyond reasoning comes.... All the different steps in yoga are intended to bring us scientifically to the superconscious state or samadhi....Just as unconscious work is beneath consciousness, so there is another work which is above consciousness, and which, also, is not accompanied with the feeling of egoism....There is no feeling of I, and yet the mind works, desireless, free from restlessness, objectless, bodiless. Then the Truth shines in its full effulgence, and we know ourselves- for Samadhi lies potential in us all- for what we truly are, free, immortal, omnipotent, loosed from the finite, and its contrasts of good and evil altogether, and identical with the Atman or Universal Soul. The Vedantists say that one may stumble into super-consciousness sporadically, without the previous discipline, but it is then impure. Their test of its purity, like our test of religion's value, is empirical: its fruits must be good for life. When a man comes out of Samadhi, they assure us that he remains 'enlightened, a sage, a prophet, a saint, his whole character changed, his life changed, illumined.' The Buddhists use the word 'samadhi' as well as the Hindus; but 'dhyana' is their special word for higher states of contemplation. There seem to be four stages recognized in dhyana. The first stage comes through concentration of the mind upon one point. It excludes desire, but not discernment or judgment: it is still intellectual. In the second stage the intellectual functions drop off, and the satisfied sense of unity remains. In the third stage the satisfaction departs, and indifference begins, along with memory and self-consciousness. In the fourth stage the indifference, memory, and self-consciousness are perfected. Just what 'memory' and 'self-consciousness' mean in this connection is doubtful. They cannot be the faculties familiar to us in the lower life. Higher stages still of

contemplation are mentioned- a region where there exists nothing, and where the meditator says: 'There exists absolutely nothing,' and stops. Then he reaches another region where he says: 'There are neither ideas nor absence of ideas,' and stops again." [5]

Theūrgia {Latin. "magic"} and ceremonial initiation led the Neophyte to a sacred study of forgotten alphabets, to a grammar of high sorcery. Ancient magic was studied, and is now best studied as a many-sided jewel – vast interpretations of shining traditions all emanating from the solitary star of an Invisible College. An early form of magic and ritual initiation practiced by the *Christiani* {Greek. "anointed ones"} in ancient Roman provinces was the ritual of *agapæ*. The Agapæ were derivations of the ancient Pagan funeral feasts and Eucharistic rites in honor of the dead.

These rites were held in cemeteries and catacombs in presence of the dead, where the mummified bodies symbolized the Christ, as the image of rising again; the image that was carried round and pointed to as a cause for festive rejoicing at the Egyptian feasts. Of these early forms of ritual, Pliny writes to Emperor Trajan: "They asserted, however, that the sum and substance of their fault or error had been that they were accustomed to meet on a fixed day before dawn and sing responsively a hymn to Christ as to a god, and to bind themselves by oath, not to some crime, but not to commit fraud, theft, or adultery, not falsify their trust, nor to refuse to return a trust when called upon to do so. When this was over, it was their custom to depart and to assemble again to partake of food--but ordinary and innocent food."

Theurgy in the early history of Islam was the "Science of the Sufis," writes el'Ghazālī, a practice that:
"aims at detaching the heart from all that is not God, and at giving to it for sole occupation the meditation of the divine being. Theory being more easy for me than practice, I read (certain books) until I understood all that can be learned by study and hearsay. Then I recognized that what pertains most exclusively to their method is just what no study can grasp, but only transport, ecstasy, and the transformation of the soul. How great, for example, is the difference between knowing the definitions of health, of satiety, with their causes and conditions, and being really healthy or filled. How different to know in what drunkenness consists,-

as being a state occasioned by a vapor that rises from the stomach, and being drunk effectively. Without doubt, the drunken man knows neither the definition of drunkenness nor what makes it interesting for science. Being drunk, he knows nothing; whilst the physician, although not drunk, knows well in what drunkenness consists, and what are its predisposing conditions. Similarly there is a difference between knowing the nature of abstinence, and being abstinent or having one's soul detached from the world could be learned neither by study nor through the ears, but solely by giving one's self up to ecstasy and leading a pious life. Reflecting on my situation, I found myself tied down by a multitude of bonds - temptations on every side. Considering my teaching, I found it was impure before God. I saw myself struggling with all my might to achieve glory and to spread my name. Then, feeling my own weakness, and having entirely given up my own will, I repaired to God like a man in distress who has no more resources. He answered, as he answers the wretch who invokes him. My heart no longer felt any difficulty in renouncing glory, wealth, and my children. So I quitted Baghdad, and reserving from my fortune only what was indispensable for my subsistence, I distributed the rest. I went to Syria, where I remained about two years, with no other occupation than living in retreat and solitude, conquering my desires, combating my passions, training myself to purify my soul, to make my character perfect, to prepare my heart for meditating on God- all according to the methods of the Sufis, as I had read of them. 'This retreat only increased my desire to live in solitude, and to complete the purification of my heart and fit it for meditation. But the vicissitudes of the times, the affairs of the family, the need of subsistence, changed in some respects my primitive resolve, and interfered with my plans for a purely solitary life. I had never yet found myself completely in ecstasy, save in a few single hours; nevertheless, I kept the hope of attaining this state. Every time that the accidents led me astray, I sought to return; and in this situation I spent ten years. During this solitary state things were revealed to me which it is impossible either to describe or to point out. I recognized for certain that the Sufis are assuredly walking in the path of God. Both in their acts and in their inaction, whether internal or external, they are illumined by the light which proceeds from the prophetic source. The first condition for a Sufi is to purge his heart entirely of all that is not God. The next key of the contemplative life consists in the humble prayers which escape from the fervent soul, and in the meditations on God in which the heart is swallowed up entirely. But in reality this is only the beginning of the Sufi life, the end of Sufism being total absorption in God. The intuitions and all that proceed are, so to speak, only the threshold for those who enter.

From the beginning, revelations take place in so flagrant a shape that the Sufis see before them, whilst wide-awake, the angels and the souls of the prophets. They hear their voices and obtain their favors. Then the transport raises from the perception of forms and figures to a degree which escapes all expression, and which no man may seek to give an account of without his words involving sin."

It is impossible to understand the history of secret societies without the profoundest knowledge of their scripting the past. Without a comprehension of the laws of nature and development of mythologies, and of ancient theurgy, we lack a reputable report of how occult knowledge birthed in ancient Egypt threaded together the Gnostic, Neo-Platonism, and Hermetic mystery traditions with Isma'ili and archaic Persian ordained truth. There is a history whispering of secret sacrifices veiled from the profane behind the walls of synagogues, mosques, temples, churches, and lodges of the Illuminati Inheritance.

Yet within the volumes of this book it would be constraining to recklessly delve into *every* mystic tradition such as Rosicrucianism, Sufism, Freemasonry, Kabbalah, Yoga, Tarot and the like that has produced recorded and viable traces of ritual initiation and occult knowledge. This book serves the reader as an account of some of the most impassioned history and occult genealogy used by the traditions represented in this treatise.

An occult genealogy can be recounted by tracing magical heredity from generation to generation, maiden to mistress, Magister to Neophyte, brother to brother. You will find in this book unnatural pathways where the living meet the dead, where oral traditions marry forgotten alphabets reaching beyond human memory where secret societies direct the marriage of history with space- time.

The Invisible College drew these rituals from archaic languages of high sorcery and cryptograms during unknown hours, where the well of prophecy deepens outside the bounds of sanity. This mystic point the Arab Adepts termed *qutub*.

Wandering wayfarers that dared enter the path of Not crossed liminal breaches of Tomorrow and Yesterday, indwelling a fate of souls.

There is no beginning with the magical in the past before Man masters the mythical; this only leads to a labyrinth, or to being lost in a mist of mystification, as soon as we are out of the bog of perverted superstitions. There were students in the College, but their intelligences became illuminated by study, to coalesce with a prudence nothing could intoxicate, and incorruptible wills in magic, taking seven or ten years to acquire. They were not degenerates, or meek scholar-practitioners, nor mere social-network mages of to-day! The ancients knew that intuition and excessive superstitions could not take the place of research, and were careful to communicate all the occult sciences they inherited to those whom they deemed worthy of limitless truth. "*Add to your faith knowledge*" was the counsel of Saint Paul.

Through the proper alignment of forgotten alphabets, ritual sacrifices, secret ciphers, the human soul attained the perfection of the alignment of millions of stars, reflecting the divine sparks of Light. The transmutability of the soul is potentially immortal. Magical praxis led the Neophyte to state of æsthesia concerning mystic experiences and levels of meta-consciousness. The ability to sense, to feel and perceive the transmutability of one's consciousness, to attain altered-states, and communicate with the dead, to accurately divine, and design systems of Occult Arte comprised the praxis of magic initiations.

From ecstasy to ecstasy, the magician cast his illusions about liminal time-space defining the gods as privative. Each integral beauty of every secret ritual and sacrifice awakened within the Neophyte the potential for the transmigration of the soul. For the College, theurgy became the axis to manipulate occult matrices and points of convergence within the world's religions. Will, desire, and belief fleshed with action. For the

College's Adepts, nothing was true, only action mattered. Thought became action for the Masters of the Temple.

Magic is a transfiguration of desire, belief, and action to obtain the means to an end. A magician is an illusionist first and always. Occultism has remained a shifting undercurrent for nameless magic bequeathed to an Invisible College. The strength of the one true Invisible College lies in concealment, never appearing throughout history in its own name, always veiled upon veils by other names and institutions. Hence, we can narrate a historic succession of secret societies and their hereditary initiations.

The Invisible College meshes folk mythologies and animism with major religious doctrines and literature. Veil upon veil beneath the shifting paradigms of occult methodologies such as Tarot, astrology, Rune lore, animistic incantations, totemism, lycanthropy, exorcism, sigil and mask magic, alchemy, yoga, necromancy, ceremonial magic, druidism, tantra and other praxes are inherited from succeeding generations of Magi.

Many of these Magi living and dead hold dear the secret rituals and sacrifices generations have bequeathed. The College curriculum, a syllabi of secret study has been kept from the undeserving and uninitiated. Art, music, literature, and ordained living beauty, align the stars with the sacred monuments for past and future students of the College to uncover alone. In the incense filled chambers of the College are whispers of secret sacrifices and exotic saturnalia long hidden in ancient grimoires, forgotten alphabets, monasteries, and libraries.

Oaths of blood and heredity have been taken by initiates to conceal the dark Artes upon the earth. The ill-fated souls whom break these oaths come to know unending nightmares in a chrysalis of scarlet shadows invoking madness. Lucky are the ones who walk away from destiny's Gift. A renaissance has led the students and Adepts of the

College to devote love, life, and lies to a rebirth of ancient Ægypt's imperial faiths, the very soul and centre of all magic.

Occult genealogies of the Invisible College have already initiated a **new order** centuries ago, kept in succession by the Lodges of Freemasonry and the Rosy Cross in the Occident. One of the most recognizable symbols in the arcane language of the Invisible College is the All-Seeing Eye, a glyph used in ancient Egyptian hieroglyphs representing the ever-watchful solar divinity of Ra, and Osiris. The All-Seeing Eye is commonly found on the obverse side of the United States one-dollar note. It symbolizes the Arcana of the Illuminati heritage, posted for all the populace to 'see' on American currency.

The All-Seeing Eye is a hieroglyph of occult knowledge embedded in radio programs, schools, universities, entertainment media, in literature children read, the music teenagers undulate to, television programs, and the World Wide Web. The web of occult sciences has submerged an entire society in the illusions cast upon them by Adepts whom design and employ technology. The slave of illusion calls himself a master of magic, failing to understand his, or her, sacred study and natural laws of primacy.

For thousands of years the Imperial light of Egypt led the world in a renaissance of sacred science, architectural & engineering advances, mathematical knowledge, and mortuary ritual. The ancient Magi and their pharaohs sought to emulate the divine precession of the stars, mimicking the stage of the gods in cultural and religious memes. Sacred monuments and mortuary rites all aligned with the rising and setting of the star, Sothis {scholars point to clues of this unidentified body as Sirius}.

The twin star Sothis symbolized in Ægyptian hieroglyphics by characters for feathers, the binary SUT-Heru {Set-Horus, the Brothers symbolized by mythic twins in Greco-Roman, Babylonian, and Biblical lore}, was the Alpha

Omega of Man's romantic occult history. The binary divine nature of the Ever-Coming Solar gods in Roman magic corresponds to IU-Pater, the Father of the Gods whose mythic formula I.A.O. is initiated by the Son {Sun}. The binary God derives from Amoun-Ra, the solar fatherhood of Egypt, greatly contested by the sons of SUT-Typhon, the immaculate Mother {Isis} who birthed the divine child.

The beginnings of the "fatherless" child spawned by the Great Dragon {usually the unmated female in mythology} are symbolized by the Tarot Trump XXI entitled "The World." This is a sigil of the Typhonian current in ancient magic directly linking this magical formula, O.A.I. {the occult formula of the Solar fatherhood reversed}, to Tarot Trump VI entitled "The Lovers."

The Sun as a star in Tarot Trump XIX represents the alchemical sciences expounded by the patrilineal Illuminati. The Tarot Trump called the "Sun" in the Rider-Waite deck has twelve solar rays emanating from it. The rays in this Tarot card correspond to the twelve signs of the Zodiac, in turn divided by thirty-six decans also {*bakiu*; Egyptian, *dekanoi*; Greek, and *drekkana*; Sanskrit}. Hence, the *udjat*, the symbol of the All-Seeing Eye of Ra ever reminds Mankind of his endeavor to mimic the abode of the gods.

The ancient Sut-Typhonians, those who adored the Mother-Child, measured their calendar in accordance with the precession of Sothis, for it was the rising and setting of Sothis that signaled the annual inundation of the sacred Nile river. The Hexagram, the Hebrew Star of David really is a sigil of two interlocking triangles {pyramids}. One upright, one inverted which beckoned Mankind to study well the Hermetic maxim, "as above, so below" seen also as a hieroglyph on the obverse side of the American dollar note.

The All-Seeing Eye is ever-watching Mankind, reminding that the gods are forever observing our secret endeavors on this blue planet. There was no death for the

36

ancient Magi, only renewal grounded in the transmutability of the soul. The first initiatory schools in ancient Egypt taught the praxes of secret mortuary rites and incantations to the god *Sût*{also *Set*, or *Sutekh*}, a deity of Hyksos responsible for the arts of warfare and victory in battles.

During the Third Intermediate Period Sutekh became associated with foreign insurgency, thus transfiguring his iconology to the arts of warfare. To the Egyptians of the lower Nile region, he was the god who 'ate the moon each month,' the jackal-headed beast who swallowed Khonsu.' and brought about lunar eclipses often seen as omens of victory in battles. The earliest statuettes of *Sût* date to 3200B.C. in Hyksos. Magi who learned the secret incantations of *Sût* unlocked the secrets of the underworld and the god of Amentet, called *Anpu* {Anubis} through a ceremony called the "Opening of the Mouth."

In the New Kingdom, Chapter 23 of the *Book of Going Forth By Day* says "my mouth is opened by Ptah; the bonds that gag my mouth have been loosed by my city-god. Thoth comes fully equipped with magic…my mouth has been parted by Ptah with this metal chisel of his with which he parted the mouths of the gods." Here, instead of Horus, the gods *Ptah* and *Tahuti* {Thoth} are mentioned. Moreover, in the Pyramid Texts, the god Sût is associated with the iron of the *adze* used to open the mouth. In the New Kingdom, texts associate the bonds obstructing the mouth with Sût.

The keys to this mortuary rite lay in the Golden Dawn teachings of the Tarot Trumps, XV "The Devil," and Trump XIX "The Sun." These Tarot Trumps and the hieroglyphic teachings contained on Golden Dawn designed decks, examine the primal forces of nature that balance death on the other side of the Kabbalistic Tree of Life. When the student gazes upon these Trump Cards, one will discover they are analogous with those of the sixth Trump "Lovers," as Adam and Eve after the Fall. Hereof are the bonds of false pride, the fatality of the material life that Neophytes balanced; flesh with spirit, mind with body, action with will.

Students of the College discussed in this chapter and in the pages of this book are the Watchers; they who taught the forgotten languages of angels, men, and demons. They are the innovators of advanced architecture, engineering science, astronomy, religion, the professors of archaic universities, pharaohs, abbots of monasteries, and silent custodians of exotic sacrifices and hidden bacchanalia. Every sacred scripture of every religious tradition speaks of the College as visiting social foundations (government, church, financial and educational institutions) during significant advancements of science, technology, and cultural development in history.

The wandering souls whom are the Inheritors of the Invisible College and the secret teachings of all ages embody the "Hermit," the ninth Trump of the Tarot. Very Honoured Frater Arthur Edward Waite, himself a distinguished Freemason, and Rosicrucian Adept of the Hermetic Order of the Golden Dawn co-designed the Rider-Waite Tarot deck. Of the Hermit as a hieroglyph of the Magi, Waite writes:

"The variation from the conventional models in this card is only that the lamp is not enveloped partially in the mantle of its bearer, who blends the idea of the Ancient of Days with the Light of the World It is a star which shines in the lantern. I have said that this is a card of attainment, and to extend this conception the figure is seen holding up his beacon on an eminence. Therefore, the Hermit is not, as Court de Gebelin explained, a wise man in search of truth and justice; nor is he, as a later explanation proposes, an especial example of experience. His beacon intimates that "where I am, you also may be." It is further a card, which is understood quite incorrectly when it is connected with the idea of occult isolation, as the protection of personal magnetism against admixture. This is one of the frivolous renderings, which we owe to Éliphas Lévi. It has been adopted by the French Order of Martinism and some of us have heard a great deal of the Silent and Unknown Philosophy enveloped by his mantle from the knowledge of the profane. In true Martinism, the significance of the term *Philosophe inconnu* was of another order. It did not refer to the intended concealment of the Instituted Mysteries, much less of their substitutes, but--like the card itself--to the truth that the Divine Mysteries secure their own protection from those who are unprepared."

38

The scholars and magisters of the Invisible College, are pillars of secret societies once flourished in Alexandria, Memphis, Ephesus, Rome, Carthage, Alamut, within the walls of Tibetan monasteries, in the gardens of Isma'ili alchemists, in the libraries of Vatican Basilicas, in Coptic abbeys, Masonic lodges, depositing their secrets in these places and in the shadows of the Great Pyramids. In the search for the divine, to reclaim the sparks of light deep within the Dark Night of the Soul, and the Templars mystic Chapel Perilous, one is always alone.

The Adepts point out the means and ways, ever illuminating the nightside valleys of the shadows of death that await each seeker. The sigil of the Hermit Tarot Trump represents not only sexual innocence and inner-wisdom but also the virginal Light. The Hermit-Magi is the custodian of the Illuminati heritage, preserving the genealogy by concealing Light from mankind in his cloak. The Light withdrawn by the Hermit reminds Mankind of his straying into spiritual darkness and seeking the Light of the Gods reflected in the stars.

Nature and life are full of ecstasies; we are here to make out the ecstasies of life and death and draw them into us forever; cultivating and hiding the mysteries beyond the night of our past. For ages, the Illuminati have donned the mask of conspiracy and confusion so that we may look fully and solemnly into the masks of nature, to see the one truth: that the Gods of the past, present, and future are still children. Mystery has been called the mother of abominations but the secret sacrifices and exotic rituals have long been masked in disinformation, delusive idealisms, schizophrenic religions, and cults of socio-political progress. Our Gods are still children, and the Watchers will return in the Last Days to consider what is worth saving.

Jihad

It is up to a new generation linked irreversibly to a global community to face an array of new global challenges. These challenges mirror the global troubles enlightened men and women of the Invisible College faced during the course of the American Experiment. Global challenges such as peak oil, violent conflagration in dictatorships and terrorist groups, the widening gap of economic disparity demand vigorous collaboration if the species is to adapt to the coming singularity in cultural conversion to a global mind frame. Many people have grown fearful with recent tremendous changes in world politics.

Shifts in a global distribution of power, the emergence of influential non-state actors, and the rise of new transnational issues to the top of the global agenda provoke fear and uncertainly, and ultranationalist "patriot" ideology hampered by absence of fact and education, clouded by entrepreneurial "conspiracy theorists." Conspiracy movements are nothing but psychological terror. These channels of fear are circulated by venture commercialists in the likes of Alex Jones, and Jordan Maxwell. This ilk which includes, Gerald Celente, David Icke, Jeff Rense, Benjamin Fulford, Leo Zagami, and Texe W. Marrs. These opportunists popularize xenophobia in an ever-increasing global society, scapegoating, and mob rule. These people are not "patriots," they are psychological terrorists expanding their commercial economic ploys.

The prodigious minds contributing throughout the centuries into the global age of wonder to the pillars of art, classics, literature, music, spiritual fraternity, and the sciences are the custodians of the Invisible College, a Cabal of erotic enlightenment and artistic understanding of the darkest depths of the human condition. They are not the intrigue of conspiracy hack "patriot" writers. It does not matter whether these histories uncovered in this book 'happened,' but that prodigious people believed in these societies, and worked to heal and illuminate good men and women.

        Jones, Icke, and other asinine personalities repeatedly cite the elite men and women in our Heritage Roll-Calls as evil characters in a global theatre-like game to abolish civil liberties. Icke in his book, *The Biggest Secret*, raves over alleged Rosicrucian plots: "*The term Rosi-Crucis was also the origin, quite obviously, of the Rosicrucians, an ancient secret society which has schemed and manipulated to ensure the reptilian bloodlines continue to occupy the positions of power.*" {Icke, David. *The Biggest Secret*. Scottsdale, AZ: Bridge of Love Publications, 1999. Pg.143 Print} Icke reveals his clear absurdity over equating Rosicrucians as reptilian overlords: "*They are variously known as the Secret Chiefs, the Hidden Masters, or the Great White Brotherhood and some researchers believe they are the force behind the creation of the Freemasons, Sufis, Knights Templar, Rosicrucians, Theosophical Society, and the Hermetic Order of the Golden Dawn. I think these people are reptilians, some of them anyway.*" {Ibid, 245}

        Conspiracy producerists, like Icke and Alex Jones unforgivably, and I suspect intentionally, confuse the historic nature of Rosicrucianism and Freemasonry. From Icke, we have this unforgivable rant speaking of King James and the Rosy Cross influence in Biblical translation: "*James knighted Francis Bacon and appointed him too many important positions, including Lord Chancellor of England. Under*

James's patronage, the Templars, Rosicrucians and other secret societies joined forces under one name, Freemasonry." {Ibid, 181} He later accuses Rosicrucians of being mind-controlling killers: "The Rosicrucians expanded the use of mind-altering drugs and the Assassins possibly got their very name from the way they employed drugs to mind control their killers." {Ibid, 294}

Alex Jones in his rants on Freemasonry is even more malicious and intentionally derogatory: *"Number one, your father is a 'porch Mason.' They're outside the house. There are three-hundred and sixty degrees of Freemasonry. Your father doesn't even know about those three-sixty. Your father only thinks there's thirty-three."* {Alex Jones Weekly Report Filmed Live November 9th, 2004} Profuse amounts of disinformation and intentionally disingenuous writings are readily available on the Internet to unsuspecting researchers. We can only surmise that the reasons for the conspiracy movement's various cliques diseducation campaign is to line their own coffers, commercializing fear and apprehension in times of social and economic disorientation.

One of the major differences between individuals who pursue and study the fine arts, classics, and common individuals in the human condition is the ability to experience the entire spectrum of existence, to adapt and change their environment according to their desire. Occultism often attracts narcissistic personalities who have a grandiose sense of self-value, and they consistently overestimate and overvalue their endowments. They exaggerate their accomplishments and are boastful, arrogant, and pretentious. Many have real talents and abilities, most are simply legends in their own mind tending not to test themselves in the natural echelons.

Their identities are codependent on their emotions, expending critical amounts of energy guarding against feelings of shame, humiliation and protecting themselves from criticism. It is not uncommon for them to be easily wounded and oscillate between guarding feelings of superiority, against having anyone finding out how inferior they feel compared to their delusions of superiority. Occult personalities, such as Crowley and his Thelemic cult, Golden Dawn personalities Griffin, Zink, and Cherubim are very status oriented and prefer to be with admirers or others who can maintain and inflate their feelings of artificial prodigy.

These megalomaniacs have a strong sense of entitlement, often denied them in professional, social, and academic environments preferring to focus their feelings on lacking qualities. They incapable of taking responsibility for their behavior while ignoring ensuing consequences and prefer to blame others for their moral and professional failures. Their poise is artificial, as they expend maximum efforts in denying, hiding, and lying about their moral failure.

Their relationships are frequently superficial. People are regarded either as a danger to their artificially superior status, or as a booster, enabling approval and serving as an audience. While they may be very good at showing concern for others, especially within a group setting, it is a sham. They lack real compassion and emotional depth, too preoccupied with their grandiose fantasies, keeping themselves from feelings of despair, sadness, and emptiness. As a rule their relationship are short and artificial.

They do not see the world clearly; because they are blinded by feelings of entitlement, and delusions of grandeur. They remain unaware of their neuroses, unaware their minds are lost in delusion. Individuals like Griffin, Breeze, and Cherubim who are in positions of artificial "influence" are quickly wounded, often silently, at the slightest perceived insult. Such perceptions descend into paranoia, and feelings of depression, aggression, and recrimination. My experiences in observance of several occult personalities like Griffin, Breeze, Cherubim, and Thelemites indicates that if these individuals do not resolve issues of entitlement they are physically unhealthy, unattractive, and unintelligent, unable to apply intelligence professionally and artistically.

Their strategies for coping moral and artistic failure is to increase their level of controlling behavior. Some become eccentric and withdraw from life into esoteric pursuits, joining occult orders and working their way up artificial magical rankings where they can verify that they are chosen, unique, and special. Some even provoke intense persecution and crucifixion of sorts to prove their grandiose neuroses. They have extreme difficulty in accepting the proposition that nature is arbitrary, capricious, and beautifully chaotic. It is difficult for them to accept themselves and life without a story of grandeur and entitlement. Hence, they attract themselves to grandiose spiritual titles or characters, such as "Grand Master," "Founder," or even "Antichrist."

Thelema is an occult philosophy centred on neo-Gnosticism, Witchcraft, hedonism, and Nietzschian will-based philosophies popularized by Edward Alexander Crowley {Aleister Crowley} around the year A.D. 1904. Copious cultish organizations have sprouted and multiplied during and after Crowley's lifetime, many of them in their own machinations professing some version of Crowley's teachings. If we exclude the deformed sense of reality that so often bleeds from questionable characters associated with the "Occult," Crowley's teachings and literature were in essence a plagiarism of Christian Gnosticism mixed with ceremonial magic, the hyper-Cynicism of Diogenes of Siope, Nietzsche's will-based philosophies and the hedonism of Francois Rabelais and Marquis D.A.F. de Sade.

All cults stem from a fundamentalism root often from within an established religious tradition. Cults can exploit and abuse members psychologically conditioning the new proselytes into a deformed sense of reality and ideologies. Cults with elaborate and often emotional means of indoctrination often manipulate and wage authoritarian mind control over members. Cults, such as Crowley's "Thelema" are communal totalistic in their organization. Individuals join because of what the group does for them - namely, fulfill and exploit unconscious psychological needs.

The human inclination for spirituality and its latency in the human genome is subject matter than I researched for years in and out of academia. The occult sciences can open one to supernatural and neurological energies, and resources unavailable to the majority of our species for nearly two-thousand years. Permanent neurological and psychological damage can easily result from engaging occult sciences, to dilettantes and the most seasoned occultists. I have personally observed occultists develop severe neuroses and psychotic complexes, and further aggravate pre-existing psychoses, by engaging in energies they could not understand nor took the time and effort to research the "dark arts."

During my studies under Dr. Hyatt's advisement, an initiated colleague, my associates and I conducted various psychological experiments and psychic invectives against various occult organizations and projects; thelemic groups O.T.O., *United Rites O.T.O.*(now defunct), Golden Dawn, *Illuminated Order of Dynamic Elements* (defunct), *Albion O.T.O.* (defunct), *Crowley Golden Dawn* (thelemic Golden Dawn; defunct, save for a scanty internet site), *Order of the Sword & Shield* (neo-Templar Order , defunct) and *Antiquities of the Illuminati*. *The purpose behind these experiments and invectives was to get a baseline measure of certain organizations and projects that have caught our attention; some of which have not been named but we contrast with the intended failures I listed*.

The experiments lasted from 2005-2007. Our initial psychological experiments resulted in probes against thelemic cults and their personalities, specifically the "*ordo templi orientis*" and its derivatives united rites O.T.O., the Crowley

45

Golden Dawn (a.k.a. *thelemic Golden Dawn*), and later the Antiquities of the Illuminati. Our invectives resulted in expected libel, threats, paranoia, and psychotic communications characteristic of thelemic and other cult worshippers. In 2006, we received many responses via the Internet, and through telephone conversations with subjects and our sources in these organizations & projects. We characterize these responses as a libelous backlash to probes of information and our denunciation of thelemic groups.

We offer as proof of collective psychotic behavior these posts from various Internet forums. The individuals behind this backlash claim to be high-ranking adepts in their respective organizations. The majority of backlash in our examination of thelema stems from psychotic individuals claiming high ranking status and 'exclusive occult knowledge'; a "David R. Jones" a high ranking member of the Ordo Templi Orientis®, a "Jeroen Hoogeweij,' a member of something called the "United Rites O.T.O.," a "Bobby Shiflett" aka 'Alamantra,' another member of the "United Rites O.T.O." and former member of the Ordo Templi Orientis® proper; and a David Wall aka "David Cherubim" an administrator of a "thelemic Golden Dawn®." Our position is that these individuals claim ranks and degrees of status in their respective groups. In addition, they insist that they each hold "illuminated" occult knowledge exclusive to humanity.

These are actual Internet posts from the individuals listed above, their supports, and our own colleagues:

• Tue Oct 17, 2006 10:28 pm
Re: [IAO-LasVegas] Re: To David Bersson
THIS PROVES THAT ALICETERION IS THE ENEMY OF THELEMA ARE YOU NOT PUBLISHING HIS BOOKS HIS PUBLISHER THINKS THELEMA IS A JOKE ALICETERION IS A LIAR ALICETERION IS THE ENEMY OF THELEMA THE STATED ENEMY OF THELEMA JOSHUA SERAPHIM SUPPORTS ALICETERION ALICETERION SUPPORTS JOSHUA SERAPHIM THE STATED ENEMY OF THELEMA ALL ENEMIES OF THELEMA WILL DIE

• Re: [AiwassThelema] Ægypt AGAIN!!!
Sat Jul 16, 2005 7:44 am
Dear Frater,
you can hardly imagine what i was put through by joshua jacob seraphim. Any influence he has must be opposed. it's not a matter of whether oai "pulls-it-off" or not. the fact is that jjs has no intention at all of leading a trip to egypt. he says, "return." His unbelievably numerous & voluminous deceptions WILL kill the Spirits of many. I may save a few. i'm glad i saved my own. AS YOU KNOW, i am not like what you describe in your uneducated reply. i do not periodically rant against jjs &/or oai. the fact is that i wouldn't even

have known about the alleged planned trip, except that another told me. near the end of 2006, he will lie about having gone--for the second time. the credulous will say, "see, he went." please understand—i WILL see Joshua Jacob Seraphim's "Carreer" in Occulture Utterly Destroyed. and, no, i'm not spending Energy on it. i only do little bits, here 'n there, when jjs offers opportunity--and when that opportunity is worth fucking with. In the Bonds of True Orders, Phoenix

• Re: [AiwassThelema] A message log about Joshua Seraphim
Thu Oct 20, 2005 12:02 pm
It's heartfelt (but in my opinion heavily unthelemic) that you are so concerned over the direction that Joshua's Will may or may not have taken him. I wasn't too surprised when I read a similar "Joshy" oriented thread of conversation in the Aiwass group. Why are you so fascinated with Joshua, his activities, whereabouts, and organisation, I mean, does it realy matter to you? Do you realy care that much? The silent Joshua may have a smile upon his face if he has been reading this thread. I hope he does! I
hope you do too, . There does seem to be a habit here of accusing unknown group members of being Joshua. Paranoid? BALSh

• Re: [AiwassThelema] digest moderation
Thu Oct 20, 2005 6:56 am
Message #378 of 1101

47

Josh has never psychologically or emotionally developed past the age of two. He tries to break anyone's toys who doesn't let him make the rules. Pretends always to be more important than he is, to the degree of inventing having an imaginary mommy that communicates to him. And tells tattling little lies about anyone he can't bully. I wonder if he still wets his bed, I'd be willing to lay long odds he does. I hear he's a closet heroin addict too and that his GF in the OAI left him when she caught him in an inapproprate situation with her 9 yr. old daughter, might be why he is macking on Kelli. It wouldn't surprise me considering the abusive type of man she is usually attracted to. It's interesting how the plot keeps thickening, and how the more Josh is exposed the more people who come forward to expose him.

• Re: [Occult Studies] Crowley and the NWO
Sat Aug 11, 2005 10:33 am
Well educated Mason. Of what Rite, of what
Degree? And for how many years in good
standing?

As My Father was a Scotish Rite Freemason of
High Degree and Good Standing for all of his
life. In a special group within that
Fraternity....They were all assasinated The
day before my 8th Birthday. And then again My
second father...assasinated on the day before
my 16th Birthday.

Your opinion I will Respect....but from
personal experience I must needs disagree with
it. And regards to those young men in this
group that have weaseled their way past the
Wardens of this Forum. Your on extreamely
precarious ground here, and you have no idea
where you are or what is around you.....leave
by the door you entered and never return. You
are woefully out of your depth here.
Doggie paddle your way back to shallower
waters. There is Leviathan lurking in the
Depths of this Sea. No servents of the Dweller

48

upon the Threshold are permitted within this
place...Leave or you will regret it to the end
of your short lived days on this planet. My
life was directly influenced by this
conspiricy crap as you call it...I spose
spending almost 20 years as a test subject for
nsa mind control and remote influencing
projects was just a figment of my overactive
imagination...

Do myself and those whom have had enough of
your "buried head in the sand" tactics and way
of life a huge service.....Blow your fucking
head off and dont breed please...I loathe the
very idea that your naive cardboard cutout
society may spread its putrid parasitic
paradigms throughout the rest of this
planetary system..let alone god forbid the
rest of this Universe. -Frater Sapere Nobelis
Astrium

• Re:[Occult Studies] Golden Dawn groups
Posted: Oct 20, 2006 3:38 PM
You insult me but honestly, you're not offending me. I couldn't
care less what a man of your status thinks of me. You have done
nothing to prove to me that you are better than I or Joshua.
Joshua has a radio show and publishes 94
books from his own company that he started BY HIMSELF. I find
that to be very respectable and more than you or I have ever done
in the public eye. You have refused to debate with Joshua over his
radio show, which only further proves your incompetence.

• Re: loser Message #1742 of 4435 >
Reply <alamantra181@> wrote: Sat Feb 24, 2007 12:21 pm
I have been trying to network with David Cherubim in order to
gain his/their assistance in directing a current against a mutual
antagonist. Please, for now, do not continue to raise current
against him or his musical project. In fact, I've asked him for
permission to use some of his material on the All Bleeding Eye. I
quickly explained to him the facts of this matter regarding the New

Falcon's/Joshua Seraphim attack, what I intended to do with the music, why I thought it, in particular, would accentuate and amplify the current we are working to raise, etc, and as of yet, haven't received a reply one way or the other. These sorts of public comments will, most likely, have a detrimental effect on my requests. Those, that some of us have decided to point a bone toward, have used magick to commit murder and have made their future intentions perfectly clear. They cannot be trifled with and we cannot squander any potential opportunity to bring their efforts to a quick close. It strikes me as being important that our designated target begin to perceive that all forces they have lashed out toward are unifying in a combined current against him ...this includes ourselves, David Cherubim, the Caliphate etc... Right now, we are diplomats and we have to be the unifying principle that organizes the various energies. This is what Magick is.

- Fwd: Hear of this?   Message #1661 of 4435
Reply
Well gentlemen, it looks like you have now attracted the attention of professional spooks ...hahahaha... good fucking luck with that one. Boy have you screwed the pooch!
<alamantra@...> wrote:
Date: Sat, 24 Feb 2007 23:57:21 -0600
Subject: [Antiquities of the Illuminati] Hear of this?
Earlier today I was sent an email from a web entity? person? group? calling itself the Dark Star Cabal. The email was an inquiry as to the blog show that Jon, Supercrip and myself have been doing called the All Bleeding Eye. The email asked me for more information about Joshua Seraphim & David Cherubim who were mentioned in the first show, and then went on to list several other names that I have never even heard of. It was signed "Causarum justia et misericordia: in camera". What is meant by in camera? Is it a request for photo evidence or something?
I ran the IP and discovered that the email was sent from McLean, Virginia. As much as I was tempted, I didn't think it best to respond to that particular email, and, in fact already deleted it and checked my harddrive for spyware, trojan horses etc. However, I was wondering if anyone on this list has heard of the Dark Star Cabal or if they have any idea what this email could be about or if anyone on this list has received a similar email. Really, strange. I thought it was kinda' "spooky" and thought it might possibly even be some cointelpro op.

In a message to the yahoo forum "Thelema93-l" dated in August 2001, a self-proclaimed follower of Aleister Crowley uses the screen name "**BinLaden93**," something that should be of interest to federal law enforcement authorities.

Message #9313 of 17857 < Prev < Prev | Next > Next >
RE: [t93] Ur-tensors; by Michael Bertiaux
Wed Aug 22, 2001   9:13 pm

Dear mr David Sharon

Do what thou wilt is the whole of the Law

As any contemporary artist can tell you, there certainly is an element of creativity involved in the process of selection (collage art, cutup technique, Koons, Warhol, Duchamps, etc etc). There are shades of suggestion involved in placing a text in a new context, that allow the viewer to look at the same piece, from another perspective.

Meaning of a text is not so much inherently in the text, but instead constructed by the reception system built around it. the text itself (ding an sich? nahhh...) is merely a small part of that system; interpretations of the biography of the author, opinions of critics, selective behaviour of publishers, reader circles etc. etc. are all determinants of the text and its ever fleeting content. If the concept interests you, I would like to refer you to my teacher on Utrecht university prof. Douwe Fokkema who even wrote a bit on the topic in the language of your tribe, which I'm sure you can find on Amazon.

Now there are open reception systems and closed reception systems. The caliphate structurally attempts to transform the Crowley corpus into a
closed reception system (attempting to control the publication, critic AND reader circle nodes), on which their crude, backwards & unhealthy 19th century mode of troglodytic 'verstehen' interpretation is projected. This is an unnatural and static state, especially when a dead author is involved, not to mention Barthes' "Death of the Author", that would actually include living authors.

51

So we have a situation here, in which a particularly cyanidic (as to avoid vitriolic) representative of an Order that preys on the remnants of a dead man, dares using the term 'creativity' against innocent bystanders ;-), let's get that straight before you continue your verbal assaults.

Your linking of this posting with any UROTO activity (we're doing fine thank you very much :-) simply proves my point. Surely Bertiaux didn't have this UROTO entity in mind when he wrote this supplemental paper. So you simply must have read another text than the one he wrote on page 356 of the Voudon Gnostic workbook. And if Bertiaux did have the UROTO in mind when he wrote that supplemental paper, then he surely won't object against manifestations of that phenomenon actually entering this particular lattice, which seems to be an activity quite harmonious with the content of the paper :o)

Love is the law, love under will
From the caves of Afghanistan,
Binladen93

"Jeroen   Hoogeweij" <binladen93@...>
binladen93@...
Send Email Messages Messages Help Message # Search:
AdvancedStart Topic
I feel left out Message List   Reply | Forward Message #896 of 901 <
Prev | Next >

Re: El ingenioso hidalgo don Quijote de la Mancha; was: Pseudo Aiwaz Experience
I experimented extensively with psychedelics until I became a father (at age 28). I tried Acid, peyote, XTC (i liked that), all kinds of mushrooms, ayahuasca, dmt, laudanum, any kind of weed and hash you can think of. The valley of Rotterdam was closely connected with the best headshop in The Netherlands (http://www.lachendepaus.nl/index_gb.html) and many traveling magicians could sell their stones, paraphernalia etc to the shop owner.
I can generate these experiences at will now, but when I was younger they were certainly interesting foreshadowings of what would come (maybe next episode ;-)

52

I take dexamphetamines as minimally as possible, smoke joints, drink coffee and enjoy an occasional laphroaig.

binladen93@...
Send Email

The Order of the Sword and Shield was founded by John P. Pirolli (*Frater Daemon Magus 777*) in February 1972 as a neo-gnostic offshoot organization mirroring the Knights Templar and Priory of Sion. Our first contact occurred in 2005 with Frater Pirolli and his representative, who offered to initiate myself via telephone, an offer I politely refused. I interviewed Mr. Pirolli via an online radio show I operated from 2005-2007 and privately communicated with him from several months, probing for information while conducting further research into the Priory of Sion mythos. The following diatribe comes from Mr. Pirolli himself in one of his Internet newsgroups:

"Posted: Aug 17, 2006 1:38 PM
Joshua Serphine (Host of Illuminati Coast to Coast), his younger sister (And Crazy Whore) Lamia, and Erika (Alleged Adult Film Actress, Typical Slut & Whore, Girlfriend of Joshua) are all working together trying to tear apart the Sword & Shield Order. They are from a Sex Cult of Lilth and want Chaos I guess? Honestly We believe that perhaps they were very envious of the Sword & Shield and it's amazing growth in the past few years and tried to bring it down as they have numerious other Magick and Mystic Orders. I guess they think anyone whose not in their little Sex Cult should be destoried. They'll get what's coming to them. We beat back others and certianly ain't afriad of these three perks. They have even tried to blackmail me, but it won't work, I'm not afriad of couple of black magick sex cerased College Students and Young Adults. The attack just caught us off guard....

Oct 21, 2006 11:35 PM
Subject: Illuminati Coast to Coast
Body: As head of the Sword and Shield I do not approve of Advertizing any shows on Illuminati Coast to Coast. Joshua Seraphim is doing his best to shut down our order. Any sword and shield member doing so will

53

be removed from the order. THIS DOES NOT APPLY TO PEOPLE
JUST IN THE THEOCOSMIC THOUGHT CENTER BUT IF YOU
ARE A MEMBER OF THE THOUGHT CENTER AND SUPPORT
THAT MAN , BE ASSURED THAT YOU'LL HAVE A SNOW BALL
CHANCE IN HELL OF BEING A MEMBER OF THE SWORD AND
SHIELD!!!!"
-Bro, 777

I will let the diatribe and its content speak for our
conclusion concerning this subject. I will not confirm or deny
the accusations against us as a college-oriented "sex cult."
The "Order of the Sword and Shield" disbanded and remains
inactive since 2007.

The "Antiquities of the Illuminati" project was an
online survey, newsgroup postings, and library archive of
articles and bibliographies related to secret societies and the
"Illuminati" mythos. The project was founded in August
1992 by Jonathan Sellers, an occultist dilettante and
California native, who uploaded the materials to the Internet
in May 2000. The project managers describe themselves as
curators of information related to secret societies and
conspiracies they refer to as "Brethren of the Gift." In their
own words:

"ON THE TERM ILLUMINATI.

After receiving a number of requests for us to explain what is meant by
the term "Illuminati," we find that it would be worth setting forth our
standards, in re the usage of the term.

Aleister Crowley, when he embarked upon the path of reforming
Magick, chose the archaic "Magic with the K" spelling of the term, in
order to set the pure science apart from the charlatan pseudo-science
that had developed into little more than a sick prank by the time in
which he found himself alive and well and writing his magnificent
tomés.

As he was given the task to rehabilitate the Science of Magick, we have been similarly instructed to revive the term Illuminati, and all it implies, namely, Illumination. Particularly from a historical context.

Similarly, for us, we have found the term Illuminati, which is a technical term, to have many sinister meanings, most of which aren't worth mentioning, as the reader will already know what we are referring to. Suffice it to say, the elusive Cabals, the Boys in the Back Room, the Secret Team, the Committees of 300, Gnomes of Zurich, Grand Druid Councils, et al, ad infinitum...

Indeed, our first acquaintance with the term was in this manner. We were cursed with having to go to a private high school, and every Tuesday they had what they referred to as "Chapel" sessions. It was a good time to catch up on missed sleep from the night before. On one such session, we were informed of this secret group that runs everything calling itself the Illuminati. They rule the world, yada yada yada, any attempt to identify them, or pursue them, or write about them, causes grief for the person with the inquiring mind.

Well, that stoked our imagination so, that eventually we had to find out what this kind of group could be. We responded to such a notion with the Bart Simpson style response, 'Cooollllll..... Nowadays, we might use the Monty Burns response, "Ex-cellll-ennnttt...'

Later, we were turned on to the various writings of Robert Anton Wilson, and that got us further involved in the mystery of what this whole thing could be.

Over time, we came to reject the notion that the rulers, the makers of policy, are the Illuminati, simply because the term, as classically understood, signifies, Enlightened Ones, Wise Ones, Wise Men, Wise Women, etc. This is not to say that the persons responsible for creating and implementing policy, or to use the Chomsky phrase, Manufacturing Consent, are stupid, or dumb, or ignint, for that matter. Indeed, they are very sharp. But the classical use of the term indicates Mystical Wisdom, SPiritual Enlightenment, the Technology of the Sacred, the Holy Doctrine.

Where does it all begin, really? With EnKi, is our answer. The original Jon, for those interested in the Johannite Tradition. For, according to the texts that have survived, EnKi established the first Order of Scientist-Priests, or Wise Men, at Eridu, thousands of years ago. These became known as the Apkallu. Several authors have written concerning the Apkallu. They are regarded as fish-men, who came out of the Persian Gulf and taught humankind the arts, sciences, agriculture, building, and so forth.

Those who are hell-bent on perpetuating the idea that the Apkallu were evil demons will tell us that they were sent by the Devil, to bring sin and worldliness into the world, and to seduce people away from the true God. To interbreed with humans, in order to create a race of half-breeds that Big Daddy hated. Of course, we are referring to pseudo researchers like David Icke, 'Branton,' William Cooper, and all the rest.

For all our travels in this gravity pit known as earth, evil comes not from spiritual sources, but is a very human thing created out of envy, fear, self-pity, shame, guilt, and so on. These are considered virtues by some people, not us. We are not going to deny that evil hierarchies exist, most certainly they do, but they are part of the plan, whereas the human evil referred to in this paragraph is something generated out of ignorance.

The historical Buddha was absolutely correct in uttering the Four

Noble Truths. Take a look around you, in American Society in particular, and you will see the truth in the Buddha's dialogues.
Now, Crowley's writings and teachings are a corrective for the Westerner in particular, as far as overcoming the disease of "sin," the diseases of envy, fear, shame, guilt, self-pity. In short, by achieving Enlightenment, by becoming Illuminated, one wakes from the sleep of ignorance. One is no longer "ignint", one has arrived at an approximation of the truth in relation to oneself.

We are told in the history books on the Illuminati, that the first usage of the term was among the Alumbrados in Spain, and the Roshiniyya in Afghanistan. That is only partially true. Far earlier than these groups, in the Languedoc region of France, in Posquiéres, in Lunel, and Narbonne, and other cities and villages, were the Maskilim. These were Jewish scholars and Sages of high renown, such as Rabbi Abraham ben David, the "RABAD"; Isaac "the Blind", and others. Gershom Scholem tells us what the term Maskilim refers to, in ORIGINS OF THE KABBALAH:

'...maskilim, a term that in philosophical circles designated the adherents of philosophical culture, whereas among the mystics it denoted the esotericists and illuminati.' -- Origins, p. 224.

We enumerated Maskilim (using the final M = 40, which may be considered white man's Kabbalah) -- and got the number 210. Consider of this. It is true that the Illuminati, for the most part, thrived and developed, not in Bavaria, but in Southern France and Northern Spain.

The Alumbrado movement came about, spread from Spain into Southern France, where this Kabbalistic element had existed already since the early 12th Century c.e., and we get groups like the Camisards of the Cevennes, the Wandering Prophets, The Illuminés. From these, eventually, we get the Illuminati of Avignon, which was established by Antoine Joseph Pernetti in the 18th century c.e., based upon the doctrines of Swedenborg, and upon Hermetica, and upon the mysteries of the locale that this group flourished in. Also, we get groups like the Philadelphes of Narbonne, who also sprang out of the same movement.

It is more likely that Weishaupt and company got their doctrines not from the near or middle east, but from the south of France, since the Order of the Bavarian Illuminati was originally organized by members of the Lodge Theodore in Munich, which received some control from the Chevaliers Bienfaisants de la Sainte Cité in Lyons. At any rate, the object, then at least, was to check the power of the Jesuits, which constituted a real threat to the cause of Freedom of Conscience, to the cause of ENlightenment in general. It still is a threat to the awakening of people from ignorance today. People who claim that the Illuminati were really secret Jesuits know not what they bark about.

IN OUR USAGE, then, we clearly identify ILLUMINATI as those who have gone before us, who have presented awareness, illumination, enlightenment, for the betterment of humankind, not to its detriment. This includes persons involved in Mysticism, Magic (and Magick), in Esoterica, Kabbalah, Islamic Mysticism, Tibetan Tantrikism, Indian Tantrikism, etc. Also, Artists, Writers, Philosophers, Scientists, Psychologists, and so forth, who have held to the paradigm, whether or not they actually belonged to some group "officially" designated as Illuminati..."

The introduction to their project and content should read as juvenile and immature at first glance, riddled with conspiracy theories, and poorly fitted pieces to a historical mystery. This theme of juvenile entitlement surfaces several times, in our probing of the AI Project. It is unfortunate Sellers and his project "managers" deteriorated over the years into paranoid behavior and delusional grandeur, especially during our probes and experiments with them. The last paragraph in their introduction agrees with the spectrum of my own research into the Illuminati heritage, to say the least of awarding credit in a field of disinformation and conspiracy producerists.

Sellers, the self-described curator behind the AI project, contracted with the late Dr. Christopher S. Hyatt and his imprint, "New Falcon Publications" in 2003 to work on the "Black Book series." Sometime in 2005, Sellers and thus his associates (as Sellers goes, so they meagerly followed) broke with Dr. Hyatt and "New Falcon Publications" over production disagreements. It is unimportant the nature of the break, what is telling is the immature and juvenile reaction by Sellers, at this point already in contact with Soror Inanna and I. Here is an exchange between Sellers and Dr. Hyatt he shares with the public:

"Jonathan Sellers <antiqillum@...> wrote: Date: Sat, 14 Oct 2006 00:53:49 -0700 (PDT)

From: Jonathan Sellers <antiqillum@...>
Subject: Re: and what nut is this one?
 To: DrHyatt@...
You are the Megalomaniac par excellence, not me.
I hate Alpha Males like yourself, AND ALWAYS HAVE.
FUCK YOUR RAMTHA FETISH!
FUCK YOU AND ALL YOUR INCOMPLETE HUMANS.
Unfortunately for YOU, you never got me. And YOU Never will. I
am no Jason Black, at 1.75 a day, now if you want someone who
fits that category I may be able to license for $1,500 a day, but I
told him to get the fuck out of my face and I hate him as much as I
hate the rest of you "wantabes" as you misspell it, bitch.
Fortunately for me, I GOT MYSELF, and I LOVE ME, and I
LOVE ME SO FUCKING MUCH THAT I SHALL GO IN AND
FUCK MYSELF ROYALLY. In you case, you can....
FUCK YOUR CRAP. GET AN ENEMA NOW! BECAUSE
YOU REALLY, REALLY NEED IT RIGHT FUCKING NOW!
AND IF YOU HAVE TO HAVE LIVE CRAP LIKE CURCIO
PROMOTING YOU, that just says a lot, now doesn't it, sweetie?
Yeah, volumes!
How IS YOUR OWN disEASE? Doctor?
7.5? I highly doubt it.........
The real spelling is "wannabe" but YOU shall always be referred
to as a "wantabe"
as per your own spelling
You people just never got it.
Time us up for all of you.
The present is NOW.
Send us $50000 and we might shut the fuck up.
But not likely.
You are like the idiot who camped in my driveway. He wouldn;t
shut up either, until I told him to get the fuck out of here.
You, Kelli, Joshua. David Cherubim (whom I met, what a fucking
worthless piece of shit he was and everybody who knows ME
knows THAT, and they know the same about you as well, now,
and the same about: Joe, Curcio, and all the rest of you are
DAMAGED GOODS, and none of you could ever write your way
out of a fucking pay toilet!

59

GET IT?

YOU HAVE BEEN ECLIPSED BY US!
WAKE UP AND REALIZE IT!
OCCULTURE IS FOR creeps and perverts
THE AUTHENTIC TRADITION is for the rest of US.
YOU PEOPLE ARE ALL LOSERS AND SHALL NEVER
ATTAIN!
This is not a drunk, this is reality speaking to you RIGHT NOW!
GO AND TAKE A FLYING FUCK AT A ROLLING DONUT,
but besure and don't take any calories, cuz that might mess up yer
blood sugar tests.....

DrHyatt@... wrote:
You have already given me permission to all that
I claim therefore you are
nothing more than a meglomaniac similiar to a JZ Knight/Ramtha.
Hows your DISease Doctor.
Matheny tells me your nothing more than a wanta be.
Welcomed to the Ninth Gate!
Enjoy what I HAVE GIVEN YOU!
Never mind the fire Mr Balken.
-d

The "Curator" of Antiquities of the Illuminati:

Even more revealing is the following diatribe by Sellers where he feels himself a successor to a "secret tradition." His exclusion of basically everyone who does not agree with him or his occult theories diminishes our hopes in a once promising project. The rants and diatribes Sellers offers to the public against Dr. Hyatt and affiliates, myself, any perceived "threat" to his "Authentic Tradition" display a severe delusion of entitlement and paranoid delusion.

[Antiquities of the Illuminati] Re: I am going to get shot here....but here it g
What people like myself are caretakers and successors of. Greenfield too. Not the Hyatts and the rest of the fly-ridden trash piles.

--- In antiquities_of_the_illuminati, "Mystery of Mysteries" <mbabalon@...> wrote:
I may sound like a complete idiot here.
What is "The Authentic Tradition"?
LVX,
M.:Babalon

--- In antiquities_of_the_illuminati@yahoogroups.com, "Alamantra" <alamantra@...> wrote:
>
> Earlier today I was sent an email from a web entity? person? group? calling itself the Dark Star Cabal. The email was an inquiry as to the blog show that Jon, Supercrip and myself have been doing called the All Bleeding Eye. The email asked me for more information about Joshua Seraphim & David Cherubim who were mentioned in the first show, and then went on to list several other names that I have never even heard of. It was signed "Causarum justia et misericordia: in camera". What is meant by in camera? Is it a request for photo evidence or something? I ran the IP and discovered that the email was sent from McLean, Virginia. As much as I was tempted, I didn't think it best to respond to that particular email, and, in fact already deleted it and checked my harddrive for spyware, trojan horses etc. However, I was

wondering if anyone on this list has heard of the Dark Star Cabal or if they have any idea what this email could be about or if anyone on this list has received a similar email. Really, strange. I thought it was kinda' "spooky" and thought it might possibly even be some cointelpro op.

Bliss:

XXXXXXXXX

www.luxocculta.org

Email From Jonathan Sellers to selected recipients sent on Dec. 1, 2006:

"Things are not exactly great here right now. Mother's starting to slip into senile dementia. I've called for my sister to come here tonight. You know that's got to be serious.

I think there's a definite concerted effort on the part of Joshua, Hyatt, Curcio and others against me and mine."

On 2/25/07, monamouroui <monamouroui@yahoo.ca> wrote:

That is spooky. I know that name. I am pretty sure they contacted me a few years ago. I'm traveling right now, but when I get back into my office on Tuesday I'll check my old emails to see if I still have it. I think though I've trashed all mails revolving around Tulbure. They had sent me a letter inquiring about Solomon Tulbure. That it was of great importance I confirm certain details about his life and where he lived. I didn't answer. Most people knew of my involvement with Tulbure from the Exposed group. In fact, I can think of a few people I'd like to start another Exposed group on, like all the jerk-off's with daggers in their eyes that come through here.

Anyway, I had received two letters asking about Tulbure. One from the Dark Star Cabal and another a few days later from someone claiming to be with a newspaper service that was looking into Tulbure and wanted to confirm information from me for an "article". The next day it was reported Tulbure was found dead; his skull crushed in. He was found beneath a highway overpass, so it was called a suicide. But most people think he was murdered. Or perhaps dark magick pushed him over the edge...literally! So now they are after Joshua Seraphim & David Cherubim ... hmmm ... should be interesting to see what follows.   ~ Sara

More diatribes against myself include reactions to one of our most controversial titles, Heritage of the Illuminati:

Reply
</group/antiquities_of_the_illuminati/post?act=reply&messageNum=17532>
Message
#17532 of 18339 < Prev
</group/antiquities_of_the_illuminati/message/17531> | Next
</group/antiquities_of_the_illuminati/message/17533>
Re: [Antiquities of the Illuminati] Re: A new um, sort of Illuminati book coming out

I was going to say it might enhance the profits, but then if prospects get to view the merchandise first...... like so much of the lesser materials to be found in the Digimobs. There is one of the later ones, btw, that has a large zip archive "American Masonic Library" which contains so much I can't repeat. Does include Pike's Liturgies for the 4-30 and his books on the Craft degrees.   Finding my Yezidi survey in one of the Digimobs was actually encouraging to me. Yes I miss my hard copy notes.
The second sentence: "Damn s.o.b." -- has to be spoken in a Groundskeeper Willy brogue!
What's so funny about him threatening to kill me and then crowing about it when my mom took the hit instead because of the vulnerabilities of her condition and then she knew exactly what was going on, who was doing it, and so forth speaks volumes. what's even funnier: when I first arrived here three years ago (how time flies!) I met some members of an Orisha community, via my pally the inscrutable Doctor Con. Whereas I had to explain my situation to people outside of Magick, he was hip to the whole thing from the start, and a few months down the road, when Hyatt took the high kick-off was rather impressed.... need i say more?
The head of the community remarked: One has to wonder what became of the Palero who did the dirty deed.
As Uncle Bill used to say a lot of people call themselves writers couldn't write themselves out of the shithouse.

I guess it beats pill testing. They have pill testing scams at the hospital (as seen on Movies and TV), and I would rather keep what's left of my liver! FOR SPECIAL OCCASIONS.

I can at least take pride in the fact that I never use spell-check.

Sure, I've missed a few here and there, and try to correct them as I go, but at least my texts don't look like they were written by the same people who make those ugly Tea Party signs, but then I don't come from Arizona. (No other Jon S, I'm not referring to your tenure in Arizona! You're a Californian thru and thru).

It's taken a lot longer to establish my base, my infrastructure Here. By the time I met up with most of you on the internet, in 2001-on I'd already had an operations center going full swing for 3 years. It took about 3 yrs to get to that position. This time it's taken longer because I've had to go from what was basically a couch surf situation to the gutter to this place. I am still laboring at finding a real home, a secure location for the Library, which I have every intention of digitizing and making available, and since archive.org

<http://archive.org> exists in this City, posterity should be possible. I'm a Taurus, I require stability.

On Tue, Dec 21, 2010 at 6:49 AM, jundeacon <jundeacon@...</group/antiquities_of_the_illuminati/ wrote:

Oh we must scan this and fill the torrents with it just to f#ck #p his profits.

Damn s o b; all I ask is 5 minutes alone with the little piece a   sh#t; just 5 minutes. Or maybe 10; what say a week with the tools of my choice.

Ya know I have always found it funny when someone threatens to kill someone else; personally I think the better threat is to make sure that they stay alive.

Keith

--- In antiquities_of_the_illuminati@yahoogroups.com </group/antiquities_of_the_illuminati/>
John Madziarczyk <j.madziarczyk@...> wrote:
I wasn't around here when all of the stuff happened, but it seems that someone who once was on the list, reportedly did some fucked up stuff, has come out with a book on the Illuminati. The book would be "Heritage of the Illuminati" by one Joseph Seraphim coming out February 11th according to Amazon.com

John M.

The final of his diatribes we offer is a most recent communiqué stating that after many years, his project "Antiquities of the Illuminati" is being scrapped from the Internet due to high costs. Perhaps the "caretaker" of the "Authentic Tradition" could have enrolled in school and pocketed scholarships & grants for his sideshow, or went out and got a job? Or at the very least asked his fellow "caretakers" to put up some money for the "expensive" 'Authentic Tradition?' Once again, the occult is a digital feeding ground for paranoid delusion, feelings of entitlement. After much objective observation by trained professionals including the late Dr. Hyatt, we can safely say Sellers and his defunct AI Project are near the top of the class for paranoia and delusions of grandeur in the occult arena.

Start Topic Message List Mon Jan 17,
AI Site going down indefinitely....
2011 11:34 am Reply   Message #17922 of 17931 < Prev | Next >

since $422/mo income does not allow me to afford renewing the hosting, and since only 3 books were sold last month, I am going to have to park the domain (or let it expire altogether) due to lack of funds, until further notice.

Thank you
Have a nice day (sneer)
The Mgt.
facme <antiqillum@...>father_acme Offline Send Email

The following is a collection of mind-raping, disturbing, and intelligence-boggling communications and letters from the Thelemic community. The common denominator with all these diatribes and the personalities hiding in anonymous personas is a common association with a cult centred on Aleister Crowley. The level of delusions of entitlement and paranoid fixation from these Internet communications is easily observable.

There is a phenomena associated with the "93 undercurrent" on the shadowy stage of secret societies. It produces a strange species of madness. When one's relations between people were very friendly this turns into a strange hostility. The individual afflicted seems perfectly rational and then suddenly changes and behaves totally irrationally and with great hostility. This happened within Crowley's organization and in every Thelemic organization since Crowley. There is the initial unity of goal-orientation within the group, there is friendship comradeship then the whole thing explodes individuals who were once honourable become scoundrels, the meek become mad dogs. The rational becomes totally insane. Friends become enemies filled with loathing and hatred for their former friends and mates.

A small brown dog came into the garden it was at first fawning and friendly suddenly it went from wagging its tail to baring its teeth and growling without any apparent cause. This is the phenomena personified. This strange crazy spirit had possessed a dog. This is most assuredly a Scorpio phenomenon. The nature of the madness in humans is the same as the dogs. People behave rationally like the dog and then suddenly turn into irrational maniacs saying the strangest things and behaving in a way conducive only to their estrangement from the group of which they are members.

That this force is 93 there is no question. The question is what possible value these phenomena can be. It destroys the very thing that created and sustained it. The result to any

Thelemic organisation is ruinous, members turn against each other with a passion that is tangible. One becomes obsessed by one's greatest weakness to the point and beyond madness, to survive one must recognize this phenomenon as the rot of one's own decaying sense of pride. How one deals with pride in the Occult defines whether one passes the ordeal or not. The mad dog in the garden is a personification of pride running amok to the bounds of masochistic martyrdom. It is a very dangerous force because it is very self-destructive.

There is pretty clearly a polarization occuring in the Thelemic community. While in part a naive romantic, I suggest that the Thelemic community is a larger group than OTO, but the Order as the organization that Crowley set up to spearhead the spread of Thelema, should be looked up to by the Thelemic community. That is part of what the Caliphate does, it leads. It leads by advocating the essential elements of Thelema such as Freedom, Independant Inititiation, Different Thoughts and Views, Contrary Opinion, etc, etc. As Thelemites it is our job to advocate this sort of thing. We don't have to agree with every one's idea, but by God, we stand for the principle that they have a right to say it. It is exactly the unpopular speach that needs protecting, not the acceptable speech.

If Crowley had ultimately admitted that Aiwass was only a fraud, and that Liber AL was nothing but a piece of lousy fiction, would thelema exist at all? That's doubtful. But Crowley would never and could never do such a thing, because his whole life's work was wrapped around the basic premise that the Cairo events had been real metaphysical interventions and that he had truly been the channel of revelation of the law of the New Aeon. So, the first thing an interested person, even a Thelemite, should wish to know is whether the story of those events in Cairo almost 100 years ago has been honestly reported.

*There are no civilians in various occult orders, Mr. *****. I'd suggest reviewing your papers.*

You know DJ, you're the same guy who threatened to spend tens of thousands of dollars to go after Ruthanne legally a couple of weeks ago. You mean to tell me that you failed to sue the Berkeley PD for permanent physical injury? Oh wait, didn't someone post that the lawyer dropped you as a defendant because you were...what was the word? Incoherent? Actually I dropped out voluntarily. Didn't have the same amount of wealth then as I have now, statute of limitations expired simple as that.

The problem many of us have had is with your ex Ruthy purporting many false and slanderous accusations and attributing them, albeit occasionally & obliquely, to you. She has publicly stated many things that are hearsay, violations of her oaths, and as a personal eyewitness to some, outright lies and falsehoods. Since you have made no effort whatsoever to distance yourself from her lies, it is sometimes hard to take much of what is said seriously. It is the problem with perjury, it is possible that some of what she has said is true, but when she has been caught in so many lies, and since you have been her purported source, and have not publicly proclaimed that what she says in your name did not come from you, we logically have to take much of it in the same tone. How do we know any of it is true, when what do know ourselves is falsely reported? If everything I know a person says is false, then I assume that much of the rest (that is unknown to me) of what they say is false as well. I give you the benefit of the doubt, as a generally honorable man (your profession notwithstanding ;-) but the fact is every time I read Ruthy's posts it reminds me of the lies that Trina spouted to the Berkeley P.D., and for which many of us suffered grievously. Luckily we take our obligations metaphorically, or both you and I would have a solemn and sacred duty to disembowel ruthy.

Tue Jan 31, 2006 5:38 am
Message #729 of 1101
Don't you think it is pathetic that you care so friggin much about yahoo lists and other online forums? Thelema does involve "idolizing" Crowley, after all, he brought it down and made it available to us. If Crowley is not worth idolizing, then the system is not worth following, for we do not then want the results which the path provides.

Posted: June 27, 2006 12:23 AM

Thelema is about the one Freedom, the Freedom to do your will -- and nothing else. *You are not given any other Freedom* save it be necessary to your will.

Posted: September 11, 2006 8:22 AM
all I tend to hear from Joshua Seraphim and his "brothers and sisters" on this forum is anti-Thelemite propaganda. I am simply curious as to why they have such an anti-Thelemic stint, I mean, apart from the fact that Crowley was a dick. They appear to be well read and intelligent, which *hopefully* means that an ad hominem argument is beneath them. Ultimately, my question is: Why all the spite?

Posted: July 5, 2006 12:30 PM
I credit Crowley, albeit not entirely for giving the world the neccessary revival of Freemasonry, Tarot, Kabbalah, Numerology, theology, mythology, and the search for exterterrestrial life. We could say that without Crowley, those above studies would never have the incorporation of our thought processes like they do today. Crowley is partly responsible for several 'cultures'..

Re: ~AiwazThelema~ digest moderation
Thu Oct 20, 2005 6:56 am
Message #378 of 1101
Josh has never psychologically or emotionally developed past the age of two. He tries to break anyone's toys who doesn't let him make the rules. Pretends always to be more important than he is, to the degree of inventing having an imaginary mommy that communicates to him. And tells tattling little lies about anyone he can't bully. I wonder if he still wets his bed, I'd be willing to lay long odds he does. I hear he's a closet heroin addict too and that his GF in the OAI left him when she caught him in an inapproprate situation with her 9 yr. old daughter, might be why he is macking on Kelli. It wouldn't surprise me considering the abusive type of man she is usually attracted to. It's interesting how the plot keeps thickening, and how the more Josh is exposed the more people who come forward to expose him.

Re: A message log about Joshua Seraphim

It's heartfelt (but in my opinion heavily unthelemic) that you are so concerned over the direction that Joshua's Will may or may not have taken him. I wasn't too surprised when I read a similar "Joshy" oriented thread of conversation in the Aiwass group. Why are you so fascinated with Joshua, his activities, whereabouts, and organisation, I mean, does it realy matter to you? Do you realy care that much? The silent Joshua may have a smile upon his face if he has been reading this thread. I hope he does! I hope you do too, . There does seem to be a habit here of accusing unknown group members of being Joshua. Paranoid? BALSh

Re: ~AiwazThelema~ Ægypt AGAIN!!!
Sat Jul 16, 2005 7:44 am
Dear Frater,
you can hardly imagine what i was put through by
joshua jacob seraphim. Any influence he has must
be opposed. it's not a matter of whether oai
"pulls-it-off" or not. the fact is that jjs has
no intention at all of leading a trip to egypt.
he says, "return." but he never went! His
unbelievably numerous & voluminous deceptions
WILL kill the Spirits of many. I may save a few.
i'm glad i saved my own. AS YOU KNOW, i am not
like what you describe in your uneducated reply.
i do not periodically rant against jjs &/or oai.
the fact is that i wouldn't even have known about
the alleged planned trip, except that another
told me. near the end of 2006, he will lie about
having gone--for the second time. the credulous
will say, "see, he went." please understand—i
WILL see Joshua Jacob Seraphim's "Carreer" in
Occulture Utterly Destroyed. and, no, i'm not
spending Energy on it. i only do little bits,
here 'n there, when jjs offers opportunity--and
when that opportunity is worth fucking with. In
the Bonds of True Orders, Phoenix

Tue Oct 17, 2006 10:28 pm
Re: [IAO-LasVegas] Re: To David Bersson

```
THIS PROVES THAT ALICETERION IS THE ENEMY OF
THELEMA
ARE YOU NOT PUBLISHING HIS BOOKS HIS PUBLISHER
THINKS THELEMA IS A JOKE ALICETERION IS A LIAR
ALICETERION IS THE ENEMY OF THELEMA THE STATED
ENEMY OF THELEMA JOSHUA SERAPHIM SUPPORTS
ALICETERION
ALICETERION SUPPORTS JOSHUA SERAPHIM THE
STATED ENEMY OF THELEMA
ALL ENEMIES OF THELEMA WILL DIE
```

When it comes to "enemies of Thelema" and an
adversary to O.T.O. and other Thelemic consortia, Kelli
Holloran has long been established as a formidable adversary
to the upper degree ranks of the O.T.O. Holloran, known by
many of her occult monikers such as Soror Hoor Amentii,
Padishah Khalifah, Soror Inanna, and countless other Internet
personas is a former member of the O.T.O., expelled for
allegedly uploading private documents to public Internet
servers. Ms. Holloran contacted a good friend and me
through the O.A.I. in Arizona. I met her for the first time in
2003 and found her a capable magician and intelligent student
of ancient religion and sociology.

Unfortunately, I later discovered through my
conversations with Ms. Holloran and Dr. Christopher S. Hyatt
that the reason behind her communications with the O.A.I.
and I was to divulge if we were an antagonist to the O.T.O. or
Dr. Hyatt's publishing ventures. We were neither. My
observations of Ms. Holloran's invectives against the O.T.O.
led me to conclude that in lieu of the abuse and harassment
she clearly experienced in the O.T.O., she became
neurotically obsessed with obstructing and criticizing O.T.O.
on the Internet. She would create and manage numerous
blogs, websites, and forums usually attracting the self-
medicating vitriol she sought, often deleting her projects
within weeks or months. Holloran's subterfuge and

insurgency against O.T.O. and other Thelemic consortia ultimately led to psychosis and delusion, even sexist and self-harming behavior.

Holloran summarizes her calamities with the O.T.O.:

If anyone wants to know why I joined the O.T.O. (American Caliphate) in 1994, it was primarily because of the /Book of the Law/. The /BOTL/ had spoken to me in a heightened state of consciousness and when a member asked me if I wanted to join (I had already been in communication with several of their members in two cities and present at functions and events) I decided that based on /The Book of the Law/ (accepting that), I would.

One of the primary tenets of the /BOTL/ that "spoke to me was *"Let the woman be girt with a sword before me."* I saw this in a statue -- it was a statue of Maat. The sword is Maat, behind that is Horus. All of these are only images of male and female.

I first noticed discrepancies of the Book of the Law with several of Crowley's writings or creations right away. Some of them may have been personal interpretations of various male O.T.O. members (my boyfriends and child's father as well as other lodge or camp masters), but the Priestess who really received me into the Order had this under control, apparently (until her untimely death).

In 1997 this Priestess, Soror Bufo, Camp Mistress of Christobel Wharton Hoopsnake Camp in Tucson, AZ. In addition, developer of animated films about the Holy Books of Thelema (unpublished) and many other profound artistic works was murdered execution style.

Read again: WAS MURDERED EXECUTION STYLE. They have never discovered her murderer. While she was not my Initiator she should have been, the person in control was a dwarfed size mini of incapability. Either way she was the Priestess of the GM, and camp mistress.

She was shot in the back of the head when a someone entered her home in Tucson and shot her (June 1997). They have never found the killer.

My boyfriend (who had asked me to join the OTO and to which I agreed as referenced above) was her boyfriend before me for 3 years. He

72

"disappeared" into thin air for months after her death. He did not even attend her wake. Various people attended it at Luna Loca cafe in Tucson. A few OTO members from Phoenix showed their support and were brethren. But, the Tucson OTO members really didn't seem to care that much. The highest degree member down there (not my boyfriend, my so-called Initiator) did not show his support and seemed to think she deserved it. I am not joking.

He was also very good friends with my ex-boyfriend "The Rapist" (who later was given a camp by the OTO for a short time called "Sun and Moon Camp"). The story as follows:

(1994)
I decide to be a priestess in their mass with the priest being the ex boyfriend "The Rapist" (later he was master of Sun and Moon camp). He never showed up to the Mass so Soror Bufo (who was murdered execution style in June 1997, 3 years later) was my priest.

(1994)
I realize there was an extreme problem with the Gnostic Mass, primarily the lack of female saints. I confront the above-mentioned "high degree" member (my initiator although I would say he was NEVER my initiator by his juvenile behavior) after a heightened state of consciousness about the lack of female saints and inquire why is Mohammed a saint. In my level of awareness I realize this person's response is a load of crap and unreasonable. Whatever anyone wants to argue (insert here) the argument is invalid as to why there are no female saints. All the way unto a gnostic interpretation in its highest -- and hence that there are no female saints is an affront to Thelema -- based on the form of gnosis and Identity. There is no protocol by which anyone can even argue this valid. And the fact by which that they desire to illustrate Aeon of Osiris (gnostic ideologies) as opposed to Aeon of Horus. It is as simple as that.

(1994-2000)
I continued to be a dues paying member but I never do another gnostic mass again..

(1995)
I took my IInd degree in around 1995 and through this discourse, I meet another guy who becomes a Camp Master (he is a camp master when I become pregnant with his child). I immediately realize after arguments and fighting that I will not be his "priestess" because the situation shows

two problems: they are not conducting themselves at all like a Profess house as described in Crowley's writing -- with treatment of pregnant women. Instead they are acting like little egotistical small phallus having jerk offs perpetrating domestic violence. And, with their little "old boys club" collaborative, I became acutely aware that they intended to keep the female ""sexually" (babylon) subversive as opposed to by "chastity" or "virginity." The control factor being the same sum game (OSIRIS).

(1995)
And on top of that -- they are controlling about their very literature.
 So the first item up for grabs is someone sending him Arte De Magica / De Arte Magica by Crowley. I see it on his computer screen and read it. He throws an alcoholic fit/rage etc., and commits violent acts against me while pregnant. He then says I'm on "bad report" and tries to expel me from his camp. None of this is professional or business - like. I leave and have many experiences beyond comprehension with the birth of my child. None of that is for public read at this time. I am living with and without the guy while he continues his OTO alcoholic rage existence in Chicago .

(1997)
Move to Chicago and involve myself in both his initiation charter papers for local members at Aum Ha and leave after some female from the camp are in my house having sex with him with my small child there, on top of the alcoholic rage/abuse I am receiving). (I Move to my own apt. in Chicago).

(1997)
I move back to Tucson. This is when Soror Bufo gets murdered execution style. Mind you, I had not talked to her since 1995 before I had my daughter and didn't know where she was at the time. I had intended to bring my daughter to meet her but I could never find out where she was. I didn't have many connections since returning to the area, except psycho stalker Initiator guy and my ex-boyfriend "The Rapist" who happened to see me in a thrift store (unless he followed me from somewhere?). And, my boyfriend, DJ at the strip club I worked at. Not really involved in the OTO, trying to raise my kid and go to college. I had some communication with the Initiator guy -- but mostly not involved because I'm working a lot. With now full on stalkeresque rapist ex-boyfriend randomly coming to my house -- I started feeling threatened.

74

(1997-98)
After she was killed, "the Rapist" started showing up at my house a lot all of a sudden. He acted very strange and withdrawn at first. I just thought it was grief but mind you previously, this same guy had strangled me and threatened to kill me in his tree house in the woods. All of this is a fact. He seemed to have bipolar disorder and act REALLY violent murder style all of a sudden mood swings. Yes, I passed out the time he strangled me. He also raped me one time and said it was because I had a "rape fantasy." I almost smashed his head in with a Horus statue sitting by my hand but I didn't because I thought I'd end up in a worse criminal situation than letting this jerk off get it over with. But I wouldn't put it past him (murder, rape, anything -- he's ultra-scary). I informed the OTO this they still gave him a camp. Anyone can challenge it but it is a fact that remains a fact.

(1998)
Why was I even hanging out with him? OUT OF FUCKING STUPIDITY. But I was. So he came over with me and my daughter there and seemed stalkerish. Yes, he was official in OTO along with his creepy Initiator friend. Right then my baby daddy (the other violent guy who was a OTO Initiator now but had given up his camp in Chicago to supposedly come and help me take care of our daughter). He came and this other OTO weird "The Rapist" /attempted murderer (and murder suspect) guy were sort of fighting. Baby daddy mad he was hanging around and I was letting him hang around because i hated baby daddy and wanted him to MOVE OUT. Why? he is violent gets drunk and threatens me. He had only been there from Chicago for 3 months at the time. The whole thing was a fight over the Gnostic Mass. Everyone wanted to do it and I was in the middle of this bizarre thing with psycho narcissists.

So one time my child's father (the alcoholic who had the initiation charter but had left his camp in Chicago) hits me in the face 10 times and goes to jail. This starts a whole OTO investigation BECAUSE I told "The rapist" ex-boyfriend who tells the Initiator who doesn't seem to care that Amy was murdered who tells the "big wigs" and the Electoral College (namely Christopher S. Hyatt) including Sabazius and other yahoos about this guy hitting me. They then try to question me and I tell them to fuck themselves I'm busy, they act like I have computer access or something and I seem to be busy--They are DEMANDING I respond to their investigation by certain days -- that by the time I could even check

75

"EMAIL" (back in 1998 mind you) the day had already been long gone. This was demanding and harassment instigated and perpetrated into a whole bunch of jerk off situations. All the way to the HIGHEST MEMBER.

For the past 12 years I have been going to school trying to get rid of two psychopathic losers and had no time for their investigation in 1998, nor internet access. Plus I need money at the time and had become homeless after this huge victimization against me: being beat by my baby daddy, being threatened to be killed by the stalker ex rapist boyfriend (both with Camp Masters and one with an Initiation Charter). I thank them for introducing me to narcissistic sociopaths who are attracted to Crowley. Look around you. I am lucky to have survived all of that. Anyone who reads that and says anything but AWE and WTF is like someone that finds a murder victim and says "Oh well" and walks on by.

I go back to the baby daddy a few times and finally move to a shelter. I go through hell with this baby daddy and the OTO tries to investigate the situation and eventually throws him out. I resign after 10001 items of MALE CRAP DOWN YOUR THROAT because I just get sick of their crap. It isn't like it ends here -- it starts here and snowballs all the way down the line. The rest of THAT story is in the "Thelema" group. This is not about OTO per se but Crowley and his works and do these thing violate the New Aeon as well as the Book of the Law? Yes. Where are these things? EGC and OTO. My experience with the OTO and resigning is written in another document.

The fact is the rituals all the way to the top are anti-female. My experiences are a PHYSICAL REPRESENTATION of what is in the higher degrees. They try to act pro-babylon (and I don't mean the OTO -- I mean CROWLEY. He wrote it). The Gnostic Mass, de Natura Deorum, art de magica and Liber Agape. It puts the female as reflection of male solar SUN. She is a moon. It's in the BOTL but they fail to realize that genders are an illusion.

BE THOU HADIT MY SECRET CENTER MY HEART AND MY TONGUE is ME. It is you. It is everyone in the Aeon of Horus. Not the Priest or the Priestess. It is not bad to have a physical representation of one's religion and call it sacred -- it is a travesty to fail to see the signs when it creates degradation of the Life force. Imposing sexuality on a female is just as oppressive as imposing chastity. Our Lady Babylon is

Our Lady of Guadalupe is Mother Mary. Any fetish of what the female should be (mother Isis or mother Babylon or mother anything) is merely someone's imposition of WHAT THE FEMALE SHOULD BE. See here's the thing: the female should be FREE. It is very clear in RA HOOR KHUIT who is a combination of Nuit and Hadit. It is not male even though Crowley seems to have used language to represent it as such. That is only his own anthropomorphisation of the god to himself. It is NOT male -- nor female. It is neither -- it contains both. The woman girt with a sword is a part of it as it is a vengeful god is part of it.

This is where the Gnostic Mass fails to grasp hold of it (the New Aeon). And, this needs a serious revision. The problem I think with the OTO (unless they have changed since I left in 2000 era vulgaris) is not that they have old aeon technologies -- but that they defend them vehemently and with a dogma and then refuse to change. Some people told me I could make more changes from within. Maybe so but I joined the Catholic church later and can do that too.... there's changes on these levels to be made EVERYWHERE. It will roll over us like a steamroller whether we like it or not. They are finally beginning to realize that nature CANNOT be controlled. And, control of nature and the female is a very central part of their old aeon tradition. No one ever likes to give up hold and power over something. And the fight will be tenuous whether you believe me or not.
Sincerely,
Soror Inanna

"Soror Inanna's" misfortunate narration offers a concise insight into the self-victimization that pervades ex cult members. Unlike her mythical namesake, "Inanna" is a generic victim severely damaged over years of abuse from not only the O.T.O. but of the worst kind - self-inflicted. Writing under a *male pseudonym*, Holloran reports the following bias on *Females and Fertility*:

Females and Fertility

Jack M. Dupras, M.A.

My theoretical model consists of the expansion of a

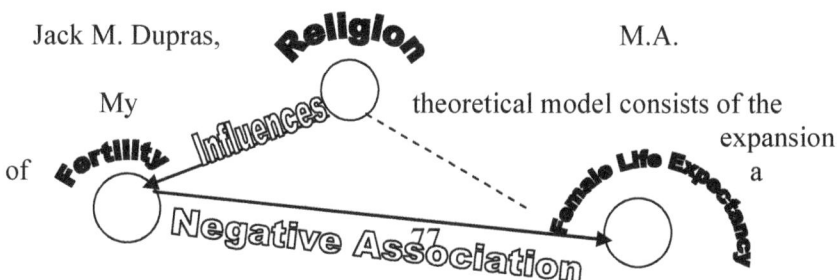

previous project which showed that fertility had a strong negative association with Female Life Expectancy. In layman's terms – more children was directly related with decreased life span for women. Included in that, I expect that by controlling for religion, fertility may increase or decrease based on "eastern" (non-Christian) vs. "western" (Christian) religious traditions. To test this, I defined "Female Life Expectancy" as the independent variable. Dependent variables were "fertility" and influencing that was also "religion."

I was unsure how the association would apply due to theories that certain religions do not allow for birth control. However, within those categories there included a wide variety of traditions, and I did not formulate the theory based on "religions which restrict birth control" to those that allow it, but along the lines of "Christian" vs. "Non Christian" (mostly western countries vs. mostly eastern countries).

I wanted to confirm or deny a cultural myth that mostly eastern countries (non-western, eastern) cause most of the world's overpopulation problems.

My Hypothesis is that Fertility has a negative association on Female Life Expectancy and Religion affects Fertility, and therefore does have an indirect effect on Female Life Expectancy.

To revise the statistical nature of my report, the conclusion is that Fertility has a strong negative association with Female Life Expectancy, but by controlling for religion (east or west) there is no significant change. What we can tell is that for every child, a woman's life is decreased by almost 5 years on average.

The results of these statistics confirm that increased fertility has a negative association with Female Life Expectancy. They also confirm that eastern (non-Christian) vs. western (Christian) religions vary in their effect but Religion itself provides no perceivably change, meaning that by controlling for the religion variable alone, predicting Female Life Expectancy by fertility stays the same.

What we can say from this is that having more children is directly correlated with dying earlier for women. One's religion or country of origin has nothing to do with it – besides perhaps one's religion informing one that having more children is beneficial. In that case, a woman may have more children based on this information rather than the facts, which are that having more children will inevitably decrease her life expectancy and cause her to die sooner.

While other invectives we presented display a clear case of malicious intent and hatred from the subjects, Soror Inanna's Internet public chronicles indicated severe characteristics of sexism, low self-esteem and neurosis towards O.T.O. and Thelema. The following chronicles originate from the forums on a fan club website to the rapper "Eminem," with whom Holloran appears obsessed, transferring her fixation and victimization onto the rapper as an idealization of her systematic criticism against O.T.O. In the following chronicle, "RHK" refers to the Thelemic deity "Ra-Hoor-Khuit:"

http://www.eminem.com/forum/default.aspx?cid=149&tid=589028
Login / Sign-up
In the Traphouse
Boards » Eminem » In the Traphouse
7/25/2011 11:12 AM (GMT-04:00)
Nellis Airforce Base (X)Nellis Airforce Base (X)

Nellis Airforce Base (X)
Joined: 5/2/2011
Posts: 2714
User Rank
Location: IR
In the Traphouse

Just because....
after doing the intense ritual to invoke RHK the guy (Jason) called (his name is jason he's a 25 yo hottie black guy wit a 9 inch dick) and then he called again when i was bawlin on the floor cuz no one loves me and just ignores me all God wants to do is leave me in the motherfuckin dirt all the time, he called me again so I said fuck it. WTF ever i was drunk already anyway from 2 Saugatuck beers. So he comes over and I dance for the guy jason and he thinks im fuckn A cuz i am obviously but whatever... and we have sex to Eminem's part in "Echo" then for like another 30 mintues when all I did the whole time was think about Eminem's ass and how he'd want that in there... BWA HAHAHAHAHAHAHAH AHAHAHAH cuz i sure didn't. Really. But like always I let the guy keep on fuckin not like he aint good or i aint good well i'm the best and he's ok as far as fucks go i just dont give a fuck and didn't wanna be fucked by then but i let the dude finish.
IT WAS THEN I DISCOVERED MY PHONE WAS MISSING and spent hours looking for the phone. I think Jason wanted to be my

homeboy living in my house and never leave even though he stole my phone on the downlow because he even let me search him a bunch of times for the phone as a sex game or something (telling me to search him) and it wasn't on him so I was freaking out and like WHERE THE FUCK IS MY PHONE and then he wanted more sex so i made him buy condoms and he smoked his last weed for a broke nigga that's all he got ... and he was pissed even though he smoked 2 blunts on me and 4 beers but whatever fucking broke ass. Then as he continued to sleep on my couch like this was the traphouse (and i was about to let it ... FUCK IT) i just got overwhelmed with my RKH rage cuz hell yea my phone was stolen the shit did not UP AND FUCKING DISAPPEAR so where is it where is it WHERE IS IT MOTHERFUCKER WHERE DID YOU PUT MY FUCKING PHONE? So he lays there more so I start yelling like GET THE HELL OUT IF I CANT HAVE MY PHONE TO TALK TO MY DAUGHTER I DONT WANNA TALK TO ANYONE and he's lik trying to calm me down like "LOOK I DONT HAVE THE PHONE YOU CAN SEARCH ME" and I'm like I DONT GIVE A FUCK IF YOU HAVE IT OR NOT I'M PISSED WITH NO PHONE NOW AND WANT YOU THE FUCK OUT OF MY HOUSE. *RIGHT NOW*

So he leaves then said he forgot his lighter so I let him in to get his lighter and he takes 5 minutes finding it and I find it finally but he's over in my dining room. Then he leaves.

Then I find this little piece of sticky two sided black plastic like you stick shit to walls with on the floor on my carpet and i realize he actually stole my phone and stuck the motherfucker under my table to get it later.

YEA I'm so fucking angry like I can afford this shit but you're happy tho cuz i fucked him and got fucked so you can smile about that cuz even when god gives me a goddamn break, he still kicks me in the heart or loins or head or somewhere to say

BUT NOT .... REALLY!!!!! HAHAHAHAH YOU LAME ASS CUNT LOVE IS A LIE! A LIE!!! THERE IS NO LOVE!!!! JUST ASK EMINEM!

Alrighty then that's my last thing I'm saying today fuck the traphouse getting some fake weed before I dance because now i know at least i can hustle and get money to sustain me until i finish my bankruptcy crap and take a few more classes to ride this student loan drip to put off the other shit and yeah a balancing act i'm in until i just cant take it anymore and fucking kill myself. Soon i hope (i get the strength to do it). I certainly already have enough sorrow to do it, just a fear of death. But I'm fastly losing confidence life is ever gonna be anything but a load of fucking bullshit for me.

You included.

http://www.eminem.com/forum/default.aspx?cid=149&tid=589561
8/2/2011 1:55 PM (GMT-04:00)
Kelli Holloran Kelli Holloran
Kelli Holloran
Joined: 8/2/2011
Posts: 5
User Rank
Location:
EMINEM OR HIS GOONS CAME INTO MY HOME AND STOLE
MY EMINEM TICKETS
EMINEM OR HIS GOONS CAME INTO MY HOME AND STOLE
MY EMINEM TICKETS WHICH I *BOUGHT* FOR FUCKING $200
AND SOLD FOR MONEY FOR MY KID'S SCHOOL CLOTHES.
NOW I HAVE TO CANCEL THE SALE AND REPORT IT TO THE
POLICE.
2 minutes ago · Privacy: · Like ·
Soror Inanna ?Lil-boosie Boosie Ardiana Bajrami Eminem Ranisha
Geter Happy Singh Marshall King Mathers Shady ltd Nikhil Mathers
Shady Records Tupac Shakur
about a minute ago · Like
Soror Inanna I CANT FUCKING BELIEVE HE DID THIS TO ME
AND ESPECIALLY MY CHILD SHE NEEDED THE FUCKING
MONEY FOR SCHOOL CLOTHES
a few seconds ago · Like
Soror Inanna I KNOW HE DID IT SPECIFICALLY BECAUSE
NOTHING *ELSE IN MY HOUSE WAS MISSING* INCLUDING MY
WALLET PHONE LAPTOP COMPUTER PRINTER AND MP3
PLAYER STEREO. I KNOW IF ANYONE FUCKING BROKE IN
THEY'D STEAL THAT SHIT TOO SO HE DID IT. HE SENT
SOMEONE TO DO IT AND NOW I HAVE NO FUCKING MONEY
TO SEND MY KID FOR HER SCHOOL CLOTHES.
2 seconds ago · Like

Eminem I dont know why
Boards » Eminem » Eminem I dont know why
8/5/2011 10:30 AM (GMT-04:00)
sororinannasororinanna
sororinanna
Joined: 3/16/2009 Posts: 6938
Eminem I dont know why

you did this to me but i am in tears. thank you for stealing the tickets i paid 200 for and also stealing the money back so now i cant even buy my kid anything and she's hating me bad and thinks i'm a fucking liar. you are breaking me down so hard and i dont really know why but it it hurts me ok you win you hurt me real bad and you hurt my kid with this. yean ill go report you to the police and court for doing this now but all this means is my kid cant buy any clothes for her to go to school.

god are you that cruel. why are you doing this to my daughter????

why.

8/5/2011 11:21 AM (GMT-04:00)
User Ranksororinannasororinanna
sororinanna
Joined: 3/16/2009
Posts: 6938
Location: UG
http://www.eminem.com/forum/default.aspx?cid=149&tid=589886
Re: Eminem I dont know why

whatever i'm gonna go get my print outs tomorrow at the box office and scalp them for cash. IDGAF you are doing this to me. YOU DID THIS. you bought them, you stole them, you reversed the payment. you cause me incredible hardship like this. I have less than $200 to my name and I'm up in here dying and you don't give a flying fuck. I try to do whatever I can to get any small amount of money while you kick your billions around like trash cans probably wasting more than i get in a month every fucking day or minute...

and then i try hard to get some cash for my little girl and you did this. why? because its Eminem tickets? i could give a fuck if its tickets to the superbowl, the olympics eminem or anything if it will get the money i need to buy my kid what she needs, and i dont have extra anything right now so i really needed it.

But its ok asshole because the more they shove me down the stronger i get. And in fact, the minute i moved in with dan he started ruining my life as fast as possible and i ended up in the YWCA for a month and the fucking homeless shelter calling section 8 like a hound from hell trying to get it back just so i could have a fucking place to live for me and my kid, and went through hell to get it back and i finally got them to give it to me and we got our apartment.

That was a lot worse than right now.

I've been broke as fuck on the greyhound in chicago before not just once so it aint nothing. You just hurt me and make it impossible for me to ever reall love you. you are doing that to yourself. me i am a hard core hustler

82

and when backed in a corner and pushed all the way to the ground i still
survive and i've done it a million times before and i'll do it again.
you are hurting me bad. you are hurting her. you are hurting our trust
with each other. i guess that's what you wanna do though huh. ruin my
relationship with my kid as much as you can.
well you're succeeding in that. but i will still get her fucking money to
her. And i will get my tickets and i will sell the motherfuckers an i will
never go watch Eminem.
FUCK YOU.

    Dr. Christopher S. Hyatt, Frater Adonai Achad, died of
cancer on February 9, 2008. Dr. Hyatt was a longtime friend
of Holloran's (Soror Inanna) and operated his own publishing
press *New Falcon Publications* since 1980 with the late Dr.
Israel Regardie, his business partner Nick Tharcher, and his
wife, Linda. After Dr. Hyatt's death., his estranged son
Michael Miller, a basketball coach at Los Angeles
Community College engaged in some ethically questionable
legal maneuvering to acquire much of the inventory and
accounts to *New Falcon Publications.*

    According to public statements given by Nick
Tharcher and Dr. Hyatt's widow; Michael Miller coerced a
terminally ill bed-ridden and incoherent Hyatt to sign Miller
to directorship of the non-profit organization, "United States
Ecclesiastical Society and Seminary," U.S.E.S.S. which
Tharcher states New Falcon Publications legally operates
under. Tharcher and Hyatt's widow resigned from New
Falcon Publications, initiated a copyright infringement
lawsuit in a United States District Court, and founded
Original Falcon Press.

    Two publishing presses began to sell the same
products and inventory, including the works of Dr. Hyatt and
Israel Regardie in the midst of copyright litigation. Each
press began "revising" Dr. Hyatt's titles, merely adding new
introductions, prefaces, and new covers. During the summer
of 2009, Holloran advised me Michael Miller of "New Falcon
Publications" wished to contract she and I to revise and

83

redesign Dr. Hyatt's world famous title, *"Undoing Yourself With Energized Meditation."* Against my better judgment I agreed and contracted with Holloran to the project. Within months we shamefully gutted much of the book, editing out articles from Hyatt's associates Michael simply did not like. We replaced all artwork at Michael Miller's instruction. To print the new edition, I discovered through the contact info Miller provided, that the printing press was simply a college and business graphics design shop, not a professional printer.

The print shop in question was a small minimum staffed shop that printed and designed college and business stationary and documents. Their printing software was not compatible with the contemporary design and publishing software Holloran and I used. Many disagreements arose because of this, giving way to unprofessional bickering from all three of us. Holloran and I removed ourselves and voided the contract.

Miller continued the project and reissued *"Undoing Yourself With Energized Meditation"* in 2010. The only contrast to previous editions of the title was merely a new cover. Original Falcon Press also issued a "revised" *"Undoing Yourself With Energized Meditation"* in 2011 also with a different cover. As of 2011, the copyright lawsuit between "Original Falcon" and "New Falcon" remains in legal purgatory. Both publishers continue to sell, revise, and recycle the exact same material save for a few new titles on ceremonial magick from the very occultists Dr. Hyatt remained distrustful towards and ruthlessly ridiculed.

We offer the following 2009 conversation via an instant messenger service between myself using the account id *"frater_annuit_coeptis"* and Holloran (Soror Inanna) who's alias in this conversation is *"aiwazthelema_tm."* The communication focuses on the difficulties of the project and personal opinions towards the "New" and "Original" Falcon

Presses. Notice Holloran's incessant obsession towards O.T.O. repeatedly resurface in the communication:

> frater_annuit_coeptis: ok...my friend wanted something
> frater_annuit_coeptis: well I have
> http://leilah.org/regardiehyatt.htm
> frater_annuit_coeptis: I will put it there too
> aiwazthelema_tm: ok i can redirect the link to there
> aiwazthelema_tm: i might be selling the books 4 him
> aiwazthelema_tm: thats the thing he is line incommunicado
> aiwazthelema_tm: he said it was a "hard fight" thanks for the support (after lon supposedly did the license to depart) and thats IT.
> frater_annuit_coeptis: pft he is letting nick and his asshole friends slander him all over
> frater_annuit_coeptis: shit
> frater_annuit_coeptis: well I don't trust him at all
> aiwazthelema_tm: i wonder what he is DOING
> frater_annuit_coeptis: I sense he is going to hand it over to nick
> aiwazthelema_tm: its not trust in my book its like
> aiwazthelema_tm: WTF are u DOING
> aiwazthelema_tm: parusing sunset strip for boys?
> aiwazthelema_tm: i suspect he is gay too
> frater_annuit_coeptis: LOL oh lord
> aiwazthelema_tm: he made 0 attempt to pick up on me yet he is entirely single
> aiwazthelema_tm: i asked him who he lives with, no one
> frater_annuit_coeptis: well he is letting them all slander him
> aiwazthelema_tm: and he's not like highly attractive that would get hollywood bimbos
> aiwazthelema_tm: he looks like alan only younger
> aiwazthelema_tm: has severe eating disorder
> aiwazthelema_tm: so i do think he may be gay
> frater_annuit_coeptis: probably
> aiwazthelema_tm: and a lot of times i called him he's with some guy in his car driving around
> frater_annuit_coeptis: damn....ugggh I am telling you I don't think he is in on this
> frater_annuit_coeptis: he is going to sell out I can sense it
> frater_annuit_coeptis: thats why i want us to act
> frater_annuit_coeptis: to salvage this!

aiwazthelema_tm: he still says he wants to build the temple though!

frater_annuit_coeptis: this all, the regardie temple, he has had no hand in this until alan died

aiwazthelema_tm: i think he wastes time money and energy doing stupid shit

frater_annuit_coeptis: yes he does

aiwazthelema_tm: picking up guys on sunset blvd or something

aiwazthelema_tm: eating out

frater_annuit_coeptis: and he is going to run regardies legacy and alan's wishes up some tweekers ass

aiwazthelema_tm: well he is bothering me with his lack of communication

aiwazthelema_tm: i will say that

aiwazthelema_tm: linda sent me a huge email this woman is a bitch

aiwazthelema_tm: they are all messed up

aiwazthelema_tm: but michael has the OTO with him

aiwazthelema_tm: the OTO is split now

frater_annuit_coeptis: ya she sent me that email for putting up excerpts of alan's work

aiwazthelema_tm: apparently bill breeze is on nicks side and lon and wasserman are on michaels

frater_annuit_coeptis: fuck the oto they are irrelevant

frater_annuit_coeptis: i think they are just doubling up, lon and wasserman to confuse us and michael

frater_annuit_coeptis: they are ALL vultures

aiwazthelema_tm: THATS WHAT I TOLD HIM

frater_annuit_coeptis: oh ... and of course he is too dumb to realize it

frater_annuit_coeptis: we need to act without him

aiwazthelema_tm: yeah

aiwazthelema_tm: well i am doing to do certain things i am preparing for buildinmg the temple at any rate

frater_annuit_coeptis: ok

frater_annuit_coeptis: same here without them

aiwazthelema_tm: it will be unfortunate if nick wins

aiwazthelema_tm: because i wont work with him

aiwazthelema_tm: i wont sell out ot him whether he wins or not

aiwazthelema_tm: i'm done with thim once he put those med records online

frater_annuit_coeptis: there is a way to beat them out

aiwazthelema_tm: b ut teh fact that breeze is working with him and he's in with the other OTO assholes

frater_annuit_coeptis: michael is too stupid to realize

aiwazthelema_tm: omfg oh did i tell u

frater_annuit_coeptis: ya

frater_annuit_coeptis: no what

aiwazthelema_tm: !!!

aiwazthelema_tm: that oto asshole that is 8=3 at that GD arizona temple nick and alan gave a charter to

aiwazthelema_tm: peter lima the one who ripped off my roman coin

aiwazthelema_tm: he found my address and started harassing me again

aiwazthelema_tm: like 2 months ago

aiwazthelema_tm: he's trying to ruin my credit / identity fraud

frater_annuit_coeptis: fuck

frater_annuit_coeptis: what did he do

aiwazthelema_tm: attemping to have books sent to my house

aiwazthelema_tm: like the "free" ones from randomhouse that send u them then send u a bill

aiwazthelema_tm: he already had about 10 magazine subscriptions sent to me that i had to cancel a few years ago

frater_annuit_coeptis: damn

frater_annuit_coeptis: ok

aiwazthelema_tm: and a box of books

frater_annuit_coeptis: fuck those people

aiwazthelema_tm: i had to ship them back or they were going to put onj my credit

aiwazthelema_tm: i have not even spoken to the guy in like 4 years

aiwazthelema_tm: he's fucking OBSESSED

frater_annuit_coeptis: wow

aiwazthelema_tm: yeah he's the webmaster for crowley's temple

aiwazthelema_tm: its on his host

aiwazthelema_tm: hes the one who designed the whole fucking site for hem

aiwazthelema_tm: them

frater_annuit_coeptis: yes i know

aiwazthelema_tm: i told michael that if he continued to associate with peter lima he was gonna be on my shit list

aiwazthelema_tm: and that he could get another web designer

aiwazthelema_tm: or i would do it

aiwazthelema_tm: and he acted like a limp lilly

aiwazthelema_tm: like peter has some kinda of hold on him

frater_annuit_coeptis: to hell with them all....he added me on myspace for some reason

aiwazthelema_tm: yeah he add drhyatt

frater_annuit_coeptis: months ago

frater_annuit_coeptis: ah ok

aiwazthelema_tm: mike crowley in and of himself is not a bad guy

aiwazthelema_tm: he's too old to know what the fuck is going on

aiwazthelema_tm: shit the guy was old back in 1990

aiwazthelema_tm: but peter lima seems to have the guy brainefucked

aiwazthelema_tm: UGH.

frater_annuit_coeptis: ya

frater_annuit_coeptis: weirdo

aiwazthelema_tm: so i have to send their temple to a shit pen because peter will likely get all the stuff

aiwazthelema_tm: i dont think michael has another person to inherit

aiwazthelema_tm: his wife took her III* OTO with me, she's on crutches

aiwazthelema_tm: cant even walk she's so overweight

aiwazthelema_tm: *thats teh one dr. hyatt was at where i first met him**

frater_annuit_coeptis: hahaha damn

aiwazthelema_tm: http://www.understandthetimes.org/newsinreview/newsinreview89.shtml#article21

frater_annuit_coeptis: hmm

aiwazthelema_tm: i dunno i regret hyatt giving them a charter

aiwazthelema_tm: peter lima started harassing me about a few weeks after alan died about it as if "that" temple is the inheritor of regardie's "lineage"

frater_annuit_coeptis: ridiculous

frater_annuit_coeptis: far from it

frater_annuit_coeptis: vultures

aiwazthelema_tm: yeah well mike crowley has NO initiatory ability at all

aiwazthelema_tm: i hung out there a bunch of times

aiwazthelema_tm: its a joke. i have his book too

frater_annuit_coeptis: no, and those who jump up to claim these things now that alan is gone are vultures

aiwazthelema_tm: alan straight up told me he thought they were a bunch of losers

aiwazthelema_tm: i mean i bet the only reason he didnt give more to us is that he juts didnt know he would die so soon

frater_annuit_coeptis: ya

aiwazthelema_tm: and so at the last minuge gave it to his son because he's better than nick

aiwazthelema_tm: in alans mind and heart anyway

frater_annuit_coeptis: ya i think so and that we were so busy i told you right before he died i had dreams...he was showing us things

aiwazthelema_tm: he even told me one time he had "something" for you and me

frater_annuit_coeptis: yeah i read that email

frater_annuit_coeptis: and....i was asking him about the IRF and he wanted us to revive it...that and he wanted to work on tantric books with us...red books or something

aiwazthelema_tm: well i could put u as a copyritgh admin but not as a owner i think

aiwazthelema_tm: or trademark admin

aiwazthelema_tm: thats all i am

frater_annuit_coeptis: thats ok for now

frater_annuit_coeptis: it will be enough for now

aiwazthelema_tm: ok i wll email him and tell him i will do it

aiwazthelema_tm: he's annoying me

frater_annuit_coeptis: but....what do you think we should do if michael does not respond

aiwazthelema_tm: i have to update it anywa

frater_annuit_coeptis: ok

aiwazthelema_tm: i dont see why he'd care

aiwazthelema_tm: he's still the owner

aiwazthelema_tm: he couldnt even figure out how to take ownership lol

frater_annuit_coeptis: well i will call him but i called him twice after christmas...no answer

frater_annuit_coeptis: thats my point!

frater_annuit_coeptis: someone has to act the copyrights are in limbo

aiwazthelema_tm: i mean i could delete teh wole thig and he woudlnt even know it frater_annuit_coeptis: he will not sue you.....he let mobius slander the hell out of him

frater_annuit_coeptis: michael is a subby...a gay sub

aiwazthelema_tm: what name should i put 4 u

aiwazthelema_tm: john r.... (?)

aiwazthelema_tm: i 4 got your real name its really long heh sorry

frater_annuit_coeptis: hmm...joshua seraphim

frater_annuit_coeptis: thats what leilah is under

aiwazthelema_tm: didnt u legally change your name?

frater_annuit_coeptis: to joshua ya

aiwazthelema_tm: ok check out the coins i got

frater_annuit_coeptis: ok

aiwazthelema_tm: to curse them curse them curse them mwahahaha

frater_annuit_coeptis: well don't give them to anyone...or the regardie cup

aiwazthelema_tm: i wont i shouldnt have given the persian one but i'm glad i did

frater_annuit_coeptis: michael will turn it over to nick i know he would

frater_annuit_coeptis: or put it on ebay

aiwazthelema_tm: it inspired me to GET THESE ONES>:)

aiwazthelema_tm: oh the ones i'm getting are far better than that one

frater_annuit_coeptis: ah ok

aiwazthelema_tm: that ones from alan and all, he bought it for me (but it was a gift to ME because of my tattoo and sorry but they cant rip my tattoo off me right)

aiwazthelema_tm: anyway mine replace that one and the one the OTO ganged

frater_annuit_coeptis: ah

aiwazthelema_tm: ganked

frater_annuit_coeptis: yeh their usual method of operation

aiwazthelema_tm: phase one: http://cgi.ebay.ca/ws/eBayISAPI.dll?ViewItem&item=380094030789

frater_annuit_coeptis: i am going to tempe the 15,16, and 17 i will turn in some trademark paperwork so we have to change it by then if possible

frater_annuit_coeptis: cool

aiwazthelema_tm: phase 2:
http://cgi.ebay.com/ws/eBayISAPI.dll?ViewItem&item=160308
719964&ssPageName=ADME:B:EOIBSA:US:1123
aiwazthelema_tm: and last and certainly not least phase 3 (for
now, theres a phase iv but i will wait until the temple is
complete)
aiwazthelema_tm:
http://cgi.ebay.com/ws/eBayISAPI.dll?ViewItem&item=310113
302561&ssPageName=ADME:B:EOIBSA:US:1123
frater_annuit_coeptis: hmm cool
aiwazthelema_tm: i'm gonna consecrate em to buildling the
temple and put them in the foundation of it
frater_annuit_coeptis: ah
aiwazthelema_tm: well i figure the persian coin was a loss but it
inspired me to get these ones so, its worth it. i would not have
been so obseessed with replacing it if i didnt
frater_annuit_coeptis: thats cool and i still have plenty of
egyptian sand....i am also ordering older edition books of
regardies and hyatts from booksellers
aiwazthelema_tm: yeah we can make the temple and get mike to
pay for it
aiwazthelema_tm: he knows nothing about magic
aiwazthelema_tm: he has some kinda blind devotion to making
the temple though i think just cuz his father wanted it
aiwazthelema_tm: i dunno how devoted he is to beating nick
though and thats bugging me ugh
frater_annuit_coeptis: i am having premonitions he is going to
sell out
frater_annuit_coeptis: i had a dream i was reading an
announcement
frater_annuit_coeptis: and there was an agreement reached out of
court
aiwazthelema_tm: nick is stating that HE has copyrights of hyatt
stuff now
aiwazthelema_tm: what the fuck
aiwazthelema_tm:
http://www.amazon.com/gp/product/1935150391/ref=olp_produ
ct_details?ie=UTF8&me=&seller=
frater_annuit_coeptis: each of them have their own distribution
accounts, michael doesn't know how to do anything related to
publishing

aiwazthelema_tm: yeah but he also dommed their website anyway
frater_annuit_coeptis: fuck it kelli...
frater_annuit_coeptis: he is worthless
aiwazthelema_tm: ok
aiwazthelema_tm: i dont know what he is doing UGHGGGGGGGG
frater_annuit_coeptis: he is fucking lazy
aiwazthelema_tm: yeah but the threat letter linda sent apparently scared his printer and his server
aiwazthelema_tm: imma update it right now
frater_annuit_coeptis: well I know what I am doing...if no one settles the regardie copyrights to hell with it all
aiwazthelema_tm: gawd this is a pain
aiwazthelema_tm: shit is saved somewhere on my computer
frater_annuit_coeptis: ok
frater_annuit_coeptis: the first thing michael should have done was establish access to their online accounts with retailers
frater_annuit_coeptis: he probably has access to any accounts they have with Abebooks, Borders, Barnes & Nobles, or any online retailer
aiwazthelema_tm: i dont see how to update it
aiwazthelema_tm: he has to sign it
aiwazthelema_tm: it has a signature form at the end
frater_annuit_coeptis: fuck him
frater_annuit_coeptis: just put your signature down as TM administrator, the owner does not have to sign it....I did it with the oai...shawna did it
frater_annuit_coeptis: or put my signature that would make more sense
aiwazthelema_tm: u there ?
frater_annuit_coeptis: yes
frater_annuit_coeptis: here
aiwazthelema_tm: ok
aiwazthelema_tm: i'm revising it
aiwazthelema_tm: i need to add all the regardie foundation dox i have
aiwazthelema_tm: do you have any
aiwazthelema_tm: my fucking cats keep deciding to sit right where my internet connex id UGH
frater_annuit_coeptis: lol hah

frater_annuit_coeptis: yes i have the complete GD....all the Regardie audio GD tapes

frater_annuit_coeptis: but a name has to be on it....yours and mine?

aiwazthelema_tm: do they say regardie foundation on em

aiwazthelema_tm: the ones u have

frater_annuit_coeptis: the complete GD pdf file does and the Regardie audios do...but i have them all as MP3s

aiwazthelema_tm: hm i cant find my damm USB

aiwazthelema_tm: wtf

frater_annuit_coeptis: oh

aiwazthelema_tm: i swear to god it like ups and fucknig goes away

aiwazthelema_tm: like akasha takes it i dunno

frater_annuit_coeptis: ha funny

aiwazthelema_tm: ahh nm its hooked to my printer lol

aiwazthelema_tm: < retard

frater_annuit_coeptis: ok

frater_annuit_coeptis: hey it is 1/11

frater_annuit_coeptis: 111

aiwazthelema_tm: u only have 1 hrs diff?

aiwazthelema_tm: oh the state

aiwazthelema_tm: date

frater_annult_coeptis: ya the date

aiwazthelema_tm: damn cat i swear waits until i'm in the middle of someting and senses PLZ SIT IN FRONT OF THE WIRELESS MODEM

frater_annuit_coeptis: cats they are jealous for attention

aiwazthelema_tm: gone now

aiwazthelema_tm: they only do it when i'm into something i swear

frater_annuit_coeptis: ha

aiwazthelema_tm: wheres your cats btw?

frater_annuit_coeptis: this girl i hooked up with in tempe before i left...she has them and when i visit her i will probably give them to my mom

aiwazthelema_tm: the motherfucker timed out

aiwazthelema_tm: i'm fucked

frater_annuit_coeptis: ya

aiwazthelema_tm: i uploaded 5 documents and now its making me start over

frater_annuit_coeptis: the uspto has like a 30min time limit aiwazthelema_tm: yeah cuz my cats disconnect my internet cosntant

aiwazthelema_tm: they did it while i was on ebay to

aiwazthelema_tm: what happen to yours ???

frater_annuit_coeptis: my what?

frater_annuit_coeptis: my cats?

aiwazthelema_tm: yeah

frater_annuit_coeptis: this girl i knew in tempe has them she liked them so i gave them to her before i left

aiwazthelema_tm: oh i thought ur mom was taking one

frater_annuit_coeptis: ya it is too cold to fly them all the way out now i have to wait until winter is over or it warms up

aiwazthelema_tm: i hope they are ok they were cuties :(

frater_annuit_coeptis: ya they are fine i talk to the girl now and then she has a nice place

frater_annuit_coeptis: you still working?

aiwazthelema_tm: yah but there is no where to change the name of the owner

frater_annuit_coeptis: hmm

aiwazthelema_tm: you cant change it

aiwazthelema_tm: did you try to do that /

frater_annuit_coeptis: on the oai yes but you might have to resubmit it, but there should be

aiwazthelema_tm: i didn't see one at all

frater_annuit_coeptis: or cancel the original app and redo it

aiwazthelema_tm: it just has the signature form thiingy at the end

aiwazthelema_tm: then i will have to repay

frater_annuit_coeptis: oh i forgot

frater_annuit_coeptis: hm

aiwazthelema_tm: just tell him to add u

frater_annuit_coeptis: fuck him

aiwazthelema_tm: i'm sure he will

aiwazthelema_tm: guh

aiwazthelema_tm: ugh

aiwazthelema_tm: he can just call the attorney and add u

aiwazthelema_tm: *sigh*

frater_annuit_coeptis: i think if you call a number they can change it for you...

aiwazthelema_tm: its making me have to sign it as the original signers

aiwazthelema_tm: its not letting me add someone or antthing

94

frater_annuit_coeptis: there should be a number you can call or something to amend it or they can help
frater_annuit_coeptis: i called a few times
frater_annuit_coeptis: its not assigned to an attorney yet so it will be easier to change once they tell you how
aiwazthelema_tm: will they email me?
frater_annuit_coeptis: yes if you email or call, or both they once helped me change things and told me what to do on the phone
aiwazthelema_tm: oh ok
aiwazthelema_tm: well you need to call him
aiwazthelema_tm: i emailed him that u wanted on the copyright
aiwazthelema_tm: TM
aiwazthelema_tm: i just said u anted to be added as a TM admin like me
frater_annuit_coeptis: yes but he is lazy
frater_annuit_coeptis: you need to contact the tm people and ask them how to change it....let them know you are the one submitting it
frater_annuit_coeptis: i could pay you but it will be dual applications...you will have to cancel the other one
aiwazthelema_tm: then they won't give it
frater_annuit_coeptis: they who
frater_annuit_coeptis: the USPTO?
aiwazthelema_tm: it will look fishy
aiwazthelema_tm: they didnt give nick new falcon
aiwazthelema_tm: UGH SOME FUCKIING OTO ASSHOLE HAS TO ACT LIKE ALAN WAS SOME HAPPY OTO MEMBER
aiwazthelema_tm: PUKE
frater_annuit_coeptis: no because he and his lawyer don't know how to do shit
aiwazthelema_tm: he admitted that
frater_annuit_coeptis: if one application is cancelled thats no problem....companies do it a lot
aiwazthelema_tm: he got a new atty
frater_annuit_coeptis: TGD even did it
frater_annuit_coeptis: nick?
frater_annuit_coeptis: well if i pay you and the other one is cancelled thats better....but you have to contact the uspto first
aiwazthelema_tm: all of my evidence shows USESS and New Falcon should have it though
frater_annuit_coeptis: USESS does not own the IRF at present?

95

frater_annuit_coeptis: and both of them are fucked up anyways...michael is a weak fool

frater_annuit_coeptis: well michael will settle out of court

frater_annuit_coeptis: and there will be no regardie legacy...oh well

aiwazthelema_tm: you'd think he'd fight more being so into sports

frater_annuit_coeptis: history will repeat itself and any trace of the irf will be swallowed up by the oto...AGAIN

frater_annuit_coeptis: well....he is gay who cares

frater_annuit_coeptis: i will pay the fee to cancel or amend the original TM app...and or create a new one

aiwazthelema_tm: i have no idea what he's doing

aiwazthelema_tm: if anything

frater_annuit_coeptis: he is not

aiwazthelema_tm: except hanging out ugh

frater_annuit_coeptis: so should i do it?

frater_annuit_coeptis: i will pay you but you have to get a hold of the uspto next week...they have an 800 number...not sure

frater_annuit_coeptis: what a fucking coincidence i am watching a movie about the Knights Templar.....a boring one

frater_annuit_coeptis: an omen

frater_annuit_coeptis: regardie and his works will be taken by templars....vampires lol

aiwazthelema_tm: har :))

frater_annuit_coeptis: don't care really

frater_annuit_coeptis: the Templars were originally ... vampire slayers!

aiwazthelema_tm: yeah i know. nick will do it until he dies then that will be it

aiwazthelema_tm: if he wins

frater_annuit_coeptis: hmm who know

aiwazthelema_tm: he wont do the regardie temple either

frater_annuit_coeptis: probably not

aiwazthelema_tm: he's just trying to make a buck off of hyatts books

frater_annuit_coeptis: yes

frater_annuit_coeptis: see what the uspto tells you...they are helpful generally

frater_annuit_coeptis: and i will pay you if they require a fee to change it...cancel...and resubmit a new one

aiwazthelema_tm: will they email me when its processed?

frater_annuit_coeptis: when what is processed? you changed it?
aiwazthelema_tm: no the application
aiwazthelema_tm: they never emailed me at all
aiwazthelema_tm: except when i first did it
aiwazthelema_tm: i added more pix i just told u
aiwazthelema_tm: thats why i think it will look stupid if i call and cancel it
aiwazthelema_tm: all my evidence shows new falcon and USESS had a history of using the IRF
aiwazthelema_tm: if i suddenly delete the app then i wll really look like a fool
aiwazthelema_tm: and what sort of evidence will i have?
frater_annuit_coeptis: no people do it all the time, companies do
frater_annuit_coeptis: copyrights and trademarks are different....once the IRF is trademarked....I will handle the copyright litigation
aiwazthelema_tm: you would be better off going on THAT one
aiwazthelema_tm: cuz i have like 8 pages of evidence
frater_annuit_coeptis: we need to trademark it first.....TMs have nothing to do with copyrights....that comes later
aiwazthelema_tm: ection 2(f), based on Evidence
The mark has become distinctive of the goods/services, as demonstrated by the attached evidence.
E2F1-24247122130-014018379_._irf2.jpg
E2F1-1-24247122130-014018379_._irf1.jpg
E2F1-24247122130-014018379_._irf5.jpg
E2F1-24247122130-014018379_._irf2-1.jpg
E2F1-24247122130-014018379_._irf2-2.jpg
E2F1-1-24247122130-014018379_._irf3.jpg
E2F1-2-24247122130-014018379_._irf4.jpg
E2F1-24247122130-014018379_._CD39_Complete_Golden_Dawn-excerpt.pdf

Section 2(f), based on Use
The mark has become distinctive of the goods/services through the applicant's substantially exclusive and continuous use in commerce for at least the five years immediately before the date of this statement.

Name(s), Portrait(s), Signature(s) of individual(s)
The name(s), portrait(s),
frater_annuit_coeptis: right right right

frater_annuit_coeptis: I just want to be listed as the owner of IRF
aiwazthelema_tm: Name(s), Portrait(s), Signature(s) of
individual(s)
The name(s), portrait(s), and/or signature(s) shown in the mark
does not identify a particular living individual.

In the original application there was an error that must be
corrected in the statement, revised as follows: In International
Class 016, the mark was first used at least as early as
01/01/1983, and first used in commerce at least as early as
01/01/1983, and is now in use in such commerce. The applicants
are submitting one specimen(s) showing the mark as used in
commerce on or in connection with any item in the class of listed
goods and/or services, consisting of a(n) These are currently (c)
U.S.E.S.S. (United States Ecclesiastical Society and Seminary)
originally Israel Regardie Foundation and Falcon Press, currently
New Falcon
frater_annuit_coeptis: the IRF and USESS are and SHOULD
BE...seperate
aiwazthelema_tm: yeah but all the evidence i submitted shows
Falcon Press, New Falcon and USESS (C) of the same books
aiwazthelema_tm: and now if i delete it and resubmit another
one it will really look fishy
frater_annuit_coeptis: no it will not...the IRF is not a publisher
aiwazthelema_tm: currently New Falcon Publications (a dba of
U.S.E.S.S.). Additionally, I have attached another printed
version of "What You Should Know About the Golden Dawn"
showing a continuing use of the mark, as well as a PDF excerpt
of U.S.E.S.S. copyright "The Complete Golden Dawn" (as the
copyright evolved from Israel Regardie Foundation to
U.S.E.S.S., the non-profit corporation submitting this
application).

frater_annuit_coeptis: AND the copyrights to many books are
NOT....NOT owned by USESS OR FALCON PRESS....many
Regardie works are REGISTERED BY THE IRF
frater_annuit_coeptis: you are combining TM rules with
Copyrights. You cannot do that.
aiwazthelema_tm: no the rest of his books are owned by
Lleywellyn
aiwazthelema_tm: llewellyn
frater_annuit_coeptis: right

frater_annuit_coeptis: and the other half....by Israel Regardie
Foundation NOT USESS
aiwazthelema_tm: thats why i think u should just get on this app
frater_annuit_coeptis: alright
frater_annuit_coeptis: so....we have to cancel or change
it....companies do it all the time....I changed my OAI app several
times
frater_annuit_coeptis: without help
aiwazthelema_tm: yeah i just did it isn't that difficult
aiwazthelema_tm: but there is no where to add a party
aiwazthelema_tm: maybe u have to do that after they have it or
something????
frater_annuit_coeptis: .....ok...well....no.
frater_annuit_coeptis: it is not assigned yet to an attorney
aiwazthelema_tm: it said owners 1 owners 2
frater_annuit_coeptis: AFTER it is assigned to an attorney it
becomes hard to change
aiwazthelema_tm: and i am not even on it
aiwazthelema_tm: just as an TM Admin
frater_annuit_coeptis: ok
aiwazthelema_tm: its USESS and Michael Miller
aiwazthelema_tm: as "CEO" of USESS
frater_annuit_coeptis: well you have to contact the uspto
BEFORE its assigned to an attorney
frater_annuit_coeptis: right now its not....so they will let you
cancel or change it
frater_annuit_coeptis: once an attorney is assigned....its complex
to do
aiwazthelema_tm: how do i tell that ?
frater_annuit_coeptis: and an attorney will be assigned.....very
soon
frater_annuit_coeptis: on the USPTO website it lists the status
frater_annuit_coeptis: TARR status
frater_annuit_coeptis: you type in israel regardie foundation and
it lists the status
frater_annuit_coeptis: once a TM is assigned an attorney....its
much harder to change things....because you have to
communicate with the assigned attorney
frater_annuit_coeptis: so....you have to do it...BEFORE an
attorney is assigned
aiwazthelema_tm: well i think michael has to do it
aiwazthelema_tm: i dont know !!!

aiwazthelema_tm: he had to call on the other one
frater_annuit_coeptis: no
frater_annuit_coeptis: what other one?
aiwazthelema_tm: he registered christopher s hyatt institute also
frater_annuit_coeptis: oh lord
frater_annuit_coeptis: ok how lame
frater_annuit_coeptis: yes but he did it not you .... you have to tell them you submitted it and it needs to change or cancel
aiwazthelema_tm: its to take the place of extreme individual institue
frater_annuit_coeptis: ooook
frater_annuit_coeptis: he has no professional credentials to run that...anyways....
frater_annuit_coeptis: YOU have to call them not michael
frater_annuit_coeptis: as the one who submitted it
frater_annuit_coeptis: if i call him and he refuses i am going to get fuckin pissed
aiwazthelema_tm: you find out how i add u as a TM admin
aiwazthelema_tm: i dont wanna spend all day on the phone at 10 cents a minute
frater_annuit_coeptis: ok
aiwazthelema_tm: i'm sure it will be fine he will email me back
frater_annuit_coeptis: well....either add me as TM admin or owner and change the whole app...ok
aiwazthelema_tm: why should he care
frater_annuit_coeptis: he does not care thats the point
aiwazthelema_tm: i will add u as that but i am not deleting the whole thing cuz look at the evidence
aiwazthelema_tm: i will really look like a damn fool
aiwazthelema_tm: my whole submission for USESS was based on that evidence as a PRE EXISTING mark
frater_annuit_coeptis: which is fine yes
frater_annuit_coeptis: thats what we want...with the IRF not USESS
frater_annuit_coeptis: we are seperating it because the IRF is the SOLE copyright registrant of regardies works....half of them
frater_annuit_coeptis: get it?
frater_annuit_coeptis: the US Copyright office does not care who the publisher is....they go by the Copyright Registrant
aiwazthelema_tm: but llewellyn will contest that!!!
aiwazthelema_tm: NF owns like 3 books
aiwazthelema_tm: or USESS/ IRF

aiwazthelema_tm: llewellyn owns the rest

frater_annuit_coeptis: no no no....we will not take Llewellyns share

aiwazthelema_tm: but heres a small ticket

frater_annuit_coeptis: right they rightfully own it

aiwazthelema_tm: the Ciceros have tons of regardie stuff that they couldnt publish since its IRF

aiwazthelema_tm: ;o)

aiwazthelema_tm: they admited it on their website

frater_annuit_coeptis: no...the USESS is not listed anywhere on the copyrights

aiwazthelema_tm: they obtained IRF shit not the copyrights to it

aiwazthelema_tm: they obtained the crap from the OTO

frater_annuit_coeptis: I know that....that comes later you are not getting it

aiwazthelema_tm: YES THEY ARE ON THE CGD

aiwazthelema_tm: ugh you dont have that one thats the issue

frater_annuit_coeptis: yes I do so....

frater_annuit_coeptis: legally what is registered with the US Copyright Office can be contested but michael doesn't care

frater_annuit_coeptis: I could put Santa Claus as copyright in a book....big deal

frater_annuit_coeptis: only the IRF is registered with the Complete GD and Audios

frater_annuit_coeptis: this is very critical and if changed....its done. period. over. another court case just to contest the claims

frater_annuit_coeptis: ok but you understand? the US Copyright Office only goes by who is listed as REGISTRANT....not what books say....contesting the claims is another bullshit headache for everyone

frater_annuit_coeptis: i have that

aiwazthelema_tm: its already been changed UGH

frater_annuit_coeptis: ?

frater_annuit_coeptis: what

frater_annuit_coeptis: where

aiwazthelema_tm: http://cocatalog.loc.gov/cgi-bin/Pwebrecon.cgi?v1=3&ti=1,3&Search_Arg=golden%20dawn&Search_Code=TALL&CNT=25&PID=mXf7QvvLo4nFPATa4 8I2DKgPv0_68&SEQ=20090111041647&SID=1

frater_annuit_coeptis: no its always been like that

frater_annuit_coeptis: nothing has changed.

frater_annuit_coeptis: you cannot tell michael about this

101

frater_annuit_coeptis: otherwise he will screw it up

frater_annuit_coeptis: or try and claim he is the grand poobah of the IRF

frater_annuit_coeptis: OF already won this gig anyways if they still have their access to distribution accounts

aiwazthelema_tm: how do you guess he's WON

frater_annuit_coeptis: having access to distribution accounts gives the public and other retailers legal recourse to do business with you

frater_annuit_coeptis: Michael is going to look weak in any legal proceeding

frater_annuit_coeptis: nick has the TM already...even though its denied they can do the necessary changes

frater_annuit_coeptis: most non-hyatt books are copyright New Falcon

frater_annuit_coeptis: and michael has little evidence he owns USESS

frater_annuit_coeptis: one signature

frater_annuit_coeptis: but nick is not contesting that

frater_annuit_coeptis: michael is assed out

frater_annuit_coeptis: no printers.....no distributors....no website....no TM....nothing...

frater_annuit_coeptis: michael does not give a shit

aiwazthelema_tm: but he is SUING nick

aiwazthelema_tm: in federal court

frater_annuit_coeptis: so he says

frater_annuit_coeptis: that will take years

aiwazthelema_tm: well i hope he is really doing something i do

frater_annuit_coeptis: i know he is not, i had a dream and read an announcement by OF that OF and michael reached an "agreement" and michael "sold" his rights or something...

frater_annuit_coeptis: i remember....OF let him do his Hyatt library and they got everything else

frater_annuit_coeptis: for a big price....thats what i was reading

aiwazthelema_tm: but in my dream they got nothing

frater_annuit_coeptis: hmm

aiwazthelema_tm: and they were ripping people off, i was getting "money" from them and they owed me 10,000 but only gave me a 20 and 80 bucks

aiwazthelema_tm: and they were ripping it off from hyatts kids

frater_annuit_coeptis: ok

frater_annuit_coeptis: everyone is ripping shit off aren't they aiwazthelema_tm: the OTO still doesnt own Gems?

frater_annuit_coeptis: don't think so

aiwazthelema_tm: look:

aiwazthelema_tm: http://www.amazon.com/Gems-Equinox-Instructions-Aleister-Crowley/dp/1578634172/ref=pd_cp_b_0?pf_rd_p=413864201&pf_rd_s=center-41&pf_rd_t=201&pf_rd_i=156184019X&pf_rd_m=ATVPDKIKX0DER&pf_rd_r=0J17TMMP1Y0M3088BWCE

frater_annuit_coeptis: thats weird

aiwazthelema_tm: look at the front page

aiwazthelema_tm: MWAHAHAHAHA

aiwazthelema_tm: OMFG

frater_annuit_coeptis: weird

aiwazthelema_tm: i looked on redwheel and they have no assn. with the IRF

frater_annuit_coeptis: right ok

frater_annuit_coeptis: well i will contact the uspto this week and see what can be done

aiwazthelema_tm: hence whoever owns it can sue them for publishign that book

aiwazthelema_tm: they can publish crowleys WRITINGS but not the organization of it or the regardie stuff!!!!

frater_annuit_coeptis: yes

frater_annuit_coeptis: so it seems

frater_annuit_coeptis: michael has no clue about publishing

frater_annuit_coeptis: i offered to help...fuck it

aiwazthelema_tm: hes not returning phone calls or emails right now either

aiwazthelema_tm: its weird because up until last sat. he was messaging me like 20 texts a day

frater_annuit_coeptis: ya

aiwazthelema_tm: when did he stop? when he met with Lon about the ocin

aiwazthelema_tm: coin

aiwazthelema_tm: i swear to fucking god

frater_annuit_coeptis: fuck him

frater_annuit_coeptis: we should do this ourselves

aiwazthelema_tm: not necesssarily

frater_annuit_coeptis: yes OF has outsold michael in the publishing industry

frater_annuit_coeptis: court will take years

frater_annuit_coeptis: i will contact the uspto anyways....just don't tell michael about what we are doing
aiwazthelema_tm: well i'm not going to delete the app
frater_annuit_coeptis: he does not have a clue what he is doing
aiwazthelema_tm: i think having USESS is stronger
frater_annuit_coeptis: not really...the usess does not own the IRF
frater_annuit_coeptis: doc separated them didn't he
frater_annuit_coeptis: michael does not give a shit
aiwazthelema_tm: more like the IRF owns usess lol
frater_annuit_coeptis: so you may have to delete it
frater_annuit_coeptis: exactly...so if it needs to be changed or deleted I will find out
aiwazthelema_tm: it should just be amended to add u lol
aiwazthelema_tm: its not a big deal
aiwazthelema_tm: imho
aiwazthelema_tm: thing is i dont think m. will do shit with it
aiwazthelema_tm: my point is to get all this crap then we run it
aiwazthelema_tm: he's about to send me all the NF books to sell
aiwazthelema_tm: i told him i'll sell them
aiwazthelema_tm: i'm not afraid of nick
aiwazthelema_tm: let him sue me
aiwazthelema_tm: i will just say they are books i own, and undercut him on amazon, ebay etc.
aiwazthelema_tm: fucking twit
aiwazthelema_tm: i can sell books if they are MINE heheh
frater_annuit_coeptis: ooook....
aiwazthelema_tm: i told michael send me the books then i will sell them and then give him the money that i dont need 4 overhead
frater_annuit_coeptis: i will find out with the uspto though
frater_annuit_coeptis: michael doesn't know shit about publishing
frater_annuit_coeptis: i know he doesn't care either
aiwazthelema_tm: i know well WE CAN RUN THE DAMN THING
aiwazthelema_tm: he can be the silent owner
aiwazthelema_tm: (and funder)
aiwazthelema_tm: which he should be cuz he doesnt wanna run it anyway but he wants the legacy cuz of his dad
aiwazthelema_tm: he told me straight up he doesnt want the responsibility of it

aiwazthelema_tm: i would do it though hell i need a job and i'd rather work from home
aiwazthelema_tm: both of us could do it we could share respondibility
aiwazthelema_tm: 1 thing tho i want the regardie temple in vegas.... near to the sekhmet one
aiwazthelema_tm: i dunno what your opinion is of that i'm sure u want it in sedona but sedona is like way overpriced
aiwazthelema_tm: that is like YEARS away tho.

Kelli Holloran / "Soror Inanna"

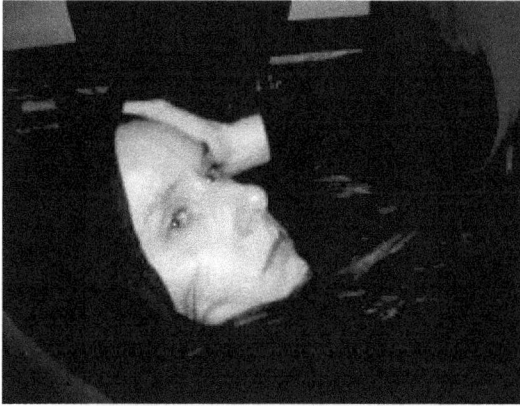

Dr. Christopher S. Hyatt's Asylum for the Insane

– On Aleister Crowley, Ordo Templi Orientis, Israel Regardie, & the Golden Dawn –

from DrHyatt@aol.com
to   Joshua.Seraphim@asu.edu
date   Mon, April 17, 2007 at 8:33 AM
subject Re: gd irf

thanks josh we got rid of all the regardie letters bb traded to some golden dawn group :::::::
if you and kelli want to develope something great::::::: cherubim bb the oto creature people:::::::::::::i hope they boil in their own shit hehehhaw:::

****
See what's free at http://www.aol.com.

DrHyatt@aol.com
by Soror Inanna on Monday, April 11, 2011 at 7:09am
DrHyatt@aol.com
 to me
show details 4/8/06

he is nuts, t hinking in the remotest fashion the oto could ever be a world influence and savior ...... of this species ...the oto is bills whoredom ...... run by the son of a sargeant ....hehehehehhe may they all eat shit and die ..... and let the worms sort them out greenfeld has missed the point, thinking in the remotest fashion the oto could ever be a world influence and savior ...... of this species ... at most the oto reflects the desperation to hold something together which has already failed at its inception— crowley's fear of abortion simply reflects his chronic fear that his inherent inferiority would be discovered .... and that his existence was a result of terrible accident .....i do applaud greenfeld's decision to step aside, not wanting to be painted with this tarnished brush ....the oto is ...... run by the son of a sargeant .... and he has applied his knowledge with complete fidelity ....the best solution to them is to ignore them ..... and let the worms sort them out

Subject: crowley-caliphate rights
DrHyatt@****" to ******
Date: Tue, 6 May 2003 14:38:13 EDT

 they bought them back a month ago, bb signed, price is confidental.....i gave the archives to oto, as a non profit so they would have a placeto live after my death, he traded them for some crowley material to a gd group, and informed me after the event ......regardies 9th was removed according to bb when crowley and fir had their fight ..... so "it would be wrong to give it back to him." even after his death...now, to be clear, bb has not thrown me out of the oto, i think he is scared, simple as that, i wish he would, it would make a nice chapter in one of my books.......under no conditions do i trust him any longer, too many lies, delays, deceit, particularly when i brought him out on my money from europe to meet with all the 9ths, i gave him the money some 1500.00 for this trip, not the oto, so i didnt claim it as a deduction...... I gave this man my loyalty and complete support and in his disgusting fashion flung me into his pile of used toys. this man makes decisions as if were god and expects everyone to find his "logic" and his notion of "fairness" without blemish ..... i was a fool. you may publish this, "dr hyatt says he was a fool for

107

supporting the oto and bb with his heart, money, love and time
.... i have been foolish in my life, but this, is on the top of my
personal stupidity " list."

Ordo Templi Orientis
'Caliphate'vot
SUBJECT: Dr. Hyatt

From: "Sabazius"
Date: Wed, 12 Feb 2003 17:17:37 -0000

To all U.S. S.G.I.G.s:
93

For your information -- as of this morning, I have suspended the
authority of Dr. Christopher Hyatt to operate as an SGIG within
the U.S., as well as his charter to initiate. The fact that Dr. Hyatt
will no longer be serving in the capacity of an S.G.I.G. or initiator
in the U.S. has been announced to the local body officers via their
announcement lists. In consideration of Dr. Hyatt's privacy, please
use due discretion in discussing this matter outside the Lover and
Hermit triads. Dr. Hyatt remains a member in good standing of the
Order.

93, 93/93
Sb

From: DrHyatt
Date: Tue, 6 May 2003 08:51:57 EDT
To: koenig at cyberlink.ch

Well Peter, is it? I took a stand on one member libeling another in
the order. the topic was over an interview i had allowed a member
to use and then he claimed it as his property, another member said
it wasnt, and the first member started calling him names in a public
forum .... i told the us kingpin that i would take the side of the

harmed member and if necessary take legal action .... the head kingpin didnt respond in any helpful manner, and i told him that i didnt recognize his authority or for that matter bb .... the us kingpin asked me if i really meant what i said, and i said yes, he asked me again, and i said yes, and again, and i said yes, so finally he "suspended me"..... the international oto boss has not done so yet, but he should as i stated clearly, that i am not taking orders from him either ...... i have donated tens of thousands of dollars to this group, promises were broken time and again, regarding my 9th as well a books, so i am done with them, they have bought back their copyrights from falcon and they have turned one of their most loyal members into a lifetime enemy .... bb also refused to give regardie back his 9th after the old mans death, and the never ending negative statements made against regardie by some of the upper boys drives me mad to no end.....
 feel free to write

Date: Wed, 7 May 2003 11:00:37 EDT

 In answer to your question regarding my "suspension" from the OTO, may i say this: I simply stated that I refuse to recognize the US King or his Boss as having authority over me....... I have been a loyal member for many years, having helped financially in a significant fashion, been an advisor helping in legal and other matters.....I was misinformed regarding a number of matters, and a number of promises made to me have been broken.......at this time I am awaiting suspension from the International OTO, overall i am now a leper in waiting having been discarded as a perpetual trouble maker..... I hope this answers your question and puts your concerns at ease...... Thank you, C.S. Hyatt, Ph.D.

Date: Wed, 7 May 2003 11:32:41 EDT

>http://www.cyberlink.ch/~koenig/dplanet/graeb3.htm

109

I have read the material you referred me to, and find nothing new there
.... i am surprised by the lack of anyone winning a lawsuit against
the OTO........and i am not suprised about how many lawsuits they win, even "defending Lon" against the bludder he made .... why so,
everytime they win, everyone loses ...... it makes them stronger ..... what is needed is something that will work, once and for all, and i suggest that you might organize such an effort ...... have any plans.... copyrights will not work .... they did everything in their power to buy falcon rights back, they did not want a suit there, and gave falcon almost complete permission to quote most anything in the future, something unheard of from bb .... his publishing venture is now the weakest spot ...... along with some items you mentioned

Date: Thu, 8 May 2003 08:01:49 EDT

first, let me inform you that i am not alturist ...... my goal in life is not to help people qua people ...... second, i hold four advanced degrees, have been a fellow at major universities and have post doc work third, i have been lic as a clinician and practiced for 12 years in addition to a two year hospital internship .... my degrees are in statistics/neruoscience/brain mapping/medical education/clinical psychology/human behavior-criminal justice ....

i have invented a statistic, which is now used, and has been published by other researchers, have written significant peer reveiwed articles, co authored and authored numerous books and have had a number of them translated into four languages.

all of this to say that i am not inticed by a public forum to protect people against the oto or any other group ... politically i might be called a libertarian....... my favorite philosopher F.W. Neitzsche who i have studied since 20, and i am now 60. by training i lean toward freud, having studied him from 17. my interest in you is

110

your knowledge about my enemy ......an enemy of my enemy is my friend ...... lon is the person who initiated me into the oto..... i was "seduced" by him, his wife, and james wasserman to join the oto......i joined because of regardie, a few years after firs death......i had a lot of fun with lon and his group......before things got serious. they wanted my name, my money, and my influence......and they got it........lon also stated that he should have been caliph.....when it came time to choose a king lon thought it would be him, but as usual bb chose someone more like him, in fact a carbon........off course bb interest in the new king had other motives which one might call the sanctury of the gnosis.....you fill in the rest. lon and i are on friendly on very distant terms...... in passing you should keep in mind that one of bb goals is to rid the order of gradys ninths having only his......most are all yes men, they are scared of him, for what reason i do not fathom .....

Date: Thu, 8 May 2003 13:18:36 EDT

BREEZE:
fruitful? helping the cause of thelema simple as that ...... i dont recall when i first met him...........somctime in the very early 90s........ are you kidding, i bought a german collection of books, numerous other items for the archives, 10s of thousands of dollars, stipends for writing books, helping pay rent, the list is never ending, donations for lawsuits etc. if you must know i was very dedicated to the cause.....

Date: Thu, 8 May 2003 17:04:10 EDT

sally quit because of a govt invest of a member of her lodge .... there were a few other heavy hitters, and some mild ones, like nick at falcon .... there are the people in europe who are more successful who have money ..... i gave him a number of 5000 stipends plus tons of other things, to help the "cause."
what is with graeb why does he need to be loved by bill and the oto .....?

111

Date: Thu, 8 May 2003 18:52:27 EDT

good night, i just received an email issued from the most high, that
everyone 5th or higher should change their password on a certain
yahoo group ...... because "peter koenig" had broken it ...... it was
not sent to me directly, but one of my friends in the oto sent it to
me ..... in passing the lodge here has been completely destroyed by
the ec, after 20 years, they sent in an sgig, other than me when i
was active, to investigate, did not inform me that "it" was here, and
then the lodge became an oasis, and then the oasis became nothing
..... non existent .... i had increased membership due to my
presence and got a 5th degree chapter besides, now they destroyed
the entire group .... in interest of the new order. interesting?

Date: Fri, 9 May 2003 09:17:57 EDT

From: "Sabazius"
Date: Wed May 7, 2003 2:39 pm
Subject: Security

93
Peter Koenig has gotten his hands on some private posts from at
least one of our OTO YahooGroups again. This would be a great
time for everyone to change their Yahoo passwords as well as their
private email account passwords.
93s
Sb

this may be in response to a scathing letter i wrote sb stating why
wasnt i copied on the my offical explusion letter .... telling him
he and his boss are experts at turning a one time loyal member and
friend into an eternal enemy ...... hehehe i also said that they are
forcing me into your hands as i learned about the original letter
from prk.......i also stated that i am waiting for bb to expell me
from the international group ..... as usual there was no response to
me apologizing for not coping me .....the phx group was destroyed
as it was in the model of the older oto when people did initations

and had fun .... strict obedience is now the rule ..... obey or else...... there are some other holes in the dyke and now is the time to create more fear in their hearts......... do your best i know you are a data collector

Who is Peter-R. Koenig?
"I need no warrant for being, and no word of sanction upon my being. I am the warrant and the sanction." - Ayn Rand

Peter-R. Koenig is a collector of data, sometimes called a gatherer of data, g.o.d. for short. He likes to solve puzzles and in particular the one sold as cOTO.....I don't know Peter well, I knew of his reputation as an evil character who was attacking the "thelemic current" of the Coto.

We first talked when he copied me on my suspension from the US CoTo. I never received a copy of the official suspension. I was simply informed that I was suspended and have lost all my powers for refusing to recognize the authority of the US Chief and of course the Grand Chief....

Prior to this I was a member in real good standing having donated thousands upon thousands of dollars to support the Coto in its defense against its enemies and to improve its library....

Somehow after throwing a number of temper tantrums for not receiving my twice promised 9th degree and eternal delays on books which I had paid stipends for completion, I was, if you would, "put aside." much like a worn set of shoes....

The once confident, advisor and supporter had worn out his welcome, however, to publicly acknowledge this could cause some embarrassing problems, and even perhaps some legal ones. But I went to sleep moving onto other things......that is until they awoke this sleeping giant.....by destroying the local lodge and then oasis, and taking the side of an individual who to say it nicely took ownership to one of my copyrighted pieces ...... with this churning my bowels I told the bosses that I no longer recognized them as authorities and after asking me three times if I really meant it, I finally said, cant you read, I received a personal notice of suspension but a never a copy of the one that went out to members of the lover and hermit triad, but wait, in order for me not to be bothered and to protect my privacy they didn't send me one, nor one to the general coto population..... kind of them?

So here comes the gather of data and sends (Peter-R. K) me a copy of this little note, designed to protect me ...... I am angry that no one had the manners to copy me ..... and thought it "clever" on how they did not want the general coto population to know, because after all I am Dr. Hyatt, a well know student of Dr. Regardie, author, etc. etc. etc. It seems that Dr., Hyatt and Dr. Regardie share more than a personal history of some 15 years, but the honor of suspended, removed, leperized by the Coto. But to be honest I have not been removed from the International Coto.....they want me to be a member for some, no doubt spiritual reason, but someone whispered in my ear that there might be more sinister reasons, I will let the reader guess what they might be ....

Prior to my suspension I was informed by the US Chief and one of his cronies that I had taken oaths to protect the Coto...they were correct, however, the Supreme Chief relieved me of these oaths, indirectly and no doubt unintentionally, when he told me that all the promises he made to me and in fact I to him were and are conditional......in my feeble way I took this to mean oaths as well, as they are promises after all......So with all of this we ask who is Peter-R. Koenig, I frankly don't know, except he is polite and friendly as he gathers data from the latest leper and victim of the COTO........some might say he is using me and I him, but what is wrong with use, when you have been misused because you believed in brotherhood, promises and the COTO...... I say mutual use is a virtue .... so for today I end my discussion of who is Peter-R. Koenig ..... but keep in mind tomorrow is another day .... I will say more........ .much more, but now the old man needs a nap.....
Thanks for listening
Dr Hyatt 5/9/03 CE

114

Dr. Christopher S. Hyatt on Dr. Francis Israel Regardie & the Golden Dawn:

Some Interesting Issues...

Before Dr. Regardie died he asked me to continue his work, particularly in the area of publishing.

Considering the ups and downs of the economy, the bankruptcy of a number of important distributors, and the general change of complexion in the industry as a whole, we give ourselves a letter grade of B. Other than the Complete Golden Dawn, demand for Dr. Regardie's work published by New Falcon has been moderate. There are a number of possible reasons.
Regardie didn't want anyone to centralize the Golden Dawn. Every one of his private students knew of this requirement. I, of course, promised that I would not attempt to control the Golden Dawn and for this I give myself a letter grade of A.

However, I can't say the same for some others, many of whom have tried to monopolize the activities of Golden Dawn as their own fiefdom. As usual they assert that they are doing it for mankind and, as usual, only fools believe such attempts at transforming greed into altruism. In my feeble attempt to counter this coup, I have created-or helped to create-functional (and dysfunctional) operating Temples. Some of these have been a practical success while others have been outright failures-as I intended them to be. However, one thing is clear: they exist and their very existence resists the attempts to "own" the Golden Dawn. For this I give myself a letter grade of B.

Even more disturbing than the attempt to monopolize the Golden Dawn is the misuse of Regardie as a steppingstone and authority.

These upstarts misused Dr. Regardie as a power base and then demeaned him. These were attempts at ad hominem character assassination. These "remarks" range from calling Regardie a fool or lacking in knowledge, to spreading rumors, to fabrications and derision surrounding the circumstances of his death. The maneuver of using a person and then demeaning him is not uncommon for individuals who lack real substance of their own.

Finally, Dr. Regardie is sometimes accused of betraying Crowley by exposing his faults in The Eye in the Triangle. Dr. Regardie's analysis of Crowley is essential to unravel the truth, as both Crowley and his followers have obfuscated an entire body of knowledge in decorative pastels. Regardie is often "hated" because, as one member of Crowley's clan has said, "How dare Regardie psychologize the prophet of the New Aeon! This is why Regardie suffered and why his reputation is questioned-this is why Crowley will be remembered and Regardie forgotten." Assertions such as these often amaze me-as their authors attempt to pass off their need for hero worship as moral imperatives. It is both funny and pathetic what a fool can do with a few footnotes. Wild assertions, academic style and clichés cannot take the place of critical thinking.

The attempt to fling Dr. Regardie to the far reaches of hell-or worse, a footnote or two-not been successful, although at times it has seemed so. Books have been published which slowly removed Regardie as a major force in the Golden Dawn, while some followers of Crowley have attempted to ignore him because Crowley and Regardie had such an awful row.

We know that the return of the Complete Golden Dawn System of Magic, in its second edition, will help bring Dr. Regardie back into the richness of the light which he so deeply deserves.

Standards, Elitism, Equality and Magic...

If you needed a heart transplant you might search for a surgeon with the best rate of success. We can define success as the highest number of patients who survived the operation, the length of time before symptoms reappeared, and possibly the quality of the patient's life after surgery. Assuming you wanted to survive, these standards-and others-might make up your selection criteria.

On the other hand, if you didn't want to survive, you would use different standards. With this idea in mind, I will conclude that no matter what you do, you have standards-and by this I include those "standards" fostered by politicians, newscasters, grammar-school teachers and derelicts. (However, if you held their "standards" you probably would have not purchased this book.)

I have standards and I assert they are based on what is defined as success, quality of life and a general feeling of well-being. I do not base my decisions or actions on what the mentally defective might do. If I have a dollar set aside for donation I will give it to a hungry genius working on the origins of life, and forego helping the inadequate. If I had two dollars I would give both to the hungry genius.

Dr. Regardie also had standards and they were not those of the "crucified one." He was an elitist and, though he sometimes failed both in judgment and results, he held to his standards nonetheless. He was kind to people, polite and concerned. However, he chose his company as carefully as he could.

Dr. Regardie donated or gave his money (and heart) to promising students in college and magic as well as to a few occult and non-occult organizations. The weak, stupid and lame were not on his donation list. He gave value to what he valued. He was not interested in the applause of bleeding-heart, guilt-ridden weaklings. One of his concerns, as is mine, are the programs designed to weaken the individual through blatant overindulgence and the teaching of self-hate which has been inculcated into the minds of the healthy and capable by a decadent morality. He fought this at every opportunity.

Elitism in this context is to support and admire the best, not the worst. This doesn't mean harming others who do not meet these standards; it simply means withholding value from them.

Dr. Regardie never attempted to reduce the best to the worst for the sake of pity. In this sense neither of us supported the politically correct notion of equality. Our attitude has led to both of us being ostracized by many occult groups-which includes most Crowley organizations. Let me make this point very clear...... Dr. Regardie was a Thelemite, something of a Jeffersonian Democrat, or a Libertarian....... However, he realized that Thelema and most political groups behaved in the exact opposite of the values and theories espoused by their founders. Although offered a high-ranking position in a number of organizations-including the OTO-he politely refused. Keep in mind that, though Dr. Regardie was a gentleman publicly, privately he could be quite vicious concerning the weak and lame who headed and populated most Occult groups.

Magic is the attempt to control paranormal or natural forces, by ritual, imagination and other techniques, to conform to the will of the operator. The term "will" in this context refers to the "force of desire." The control of paranormal forces can mean learning from "higher powers" to finding the right mate. Some individuals regard some forms of magic as either black or white. Apparently this means that black magic correlates with self-interest and harming others, while white magic relates to spiritual pursuits and helping others. Magic, however, is magic, regardless of what ends one pursues or how you might moralize about the means used to accomplish the end. Like science, magic must remain amoral-uninfluenced by any set of standards except knowledge and results.. ....

In summary, Regardie espoused the theory that, like science, magic was an objective practice...... the ritual either accomplished its ends or not.. ....

Though Regardie was a generous and caring person, he never regarded his personal values from a moral perspective nor demanded that others behave like himself.

Dr. Regardie had very high standards although, like all of us, he often failed at realizing them.. . He was a strong advocate of elitism and was horrified by what I now call the new age plague.. .... .which has distorted and obfuscated magic and science through a neopuritanical ethic, eulogized through a greatly watered down Judeo/Christian/Islamic morality.. .... The ethic of the new age, which in my view is now dwindling, is a combination of regressive self-indulgence and self-hate.. ... .two programs of self-destruction whose time has come and gone. We are now moving into a new era, neither better nor worse than the one we are emerging from.. .... This is not the so-called Aeon of Horus, but another.. .... The Aeon of Horus has come and gone in an instant and, like all minor influences, has left behind its refuse. With all of this said, we at Falcon hope that you find this new edition both more useful and enjoyable.

-Christopher S. Hyatt, Ph.D.
17 November 2002 CE
St. Thomas, USVI

"crowley's fear of abortion simply reflects his chronic fear that his inherent inferiority would be discovered .... and that his existence was a result of terrible accident ..."
Christopher S. Hyatt, Ph.D. April 8, 2006.

The Order of Myspace: A collage of lunatic cyber-
magicians.

Mosque of Thelema

In the psychology of cult behavior, emulation is an insidious form of flattery...

𝔗𝔥𝔢 𝔐𝔬𝔰𝔮𝔲𝔢 𝔬𝔣 𝔖𝔞𝔱𝔞𝔫

Founded Anno CIII
Walpurgisnacht, April 30th, 2007
era vulgari

By
Aliana XCIII

with minor assistance from

ALEISTERION

Manifesto of the Mosque

The Mosque of Satan is an institution dedicated to Shi'a Thelema, a Satanic branch of Thelema that breaks from traditional Thelemic religion and treads altogether new ground.

The Mosque believes that there is no god, i.e. we don't worship Satan: we invoke into ourselves the idea that is Satan. Our primary belief is in an impersonal force within the collective human/animal unconscious, called ShT (Hebrew *Shin Teth*) or Satan, equivalent to ourselves, and its complement, the feminine archetype, called Babylon or Babalon, the Whore of Whores. "Whore" is to us a word of honor, signifying a woman who is, while every bit a lady, also sexually liberated and promiscuous as her men are. These, it is to be noted, are not objectively real beings in any personal sense, but in fact represent the ultimate source and origin of all animal consciousness; i.e. we do not engage in any kind of slavish worship. We are ourselves the manifestation of these contrary yet complementary forces of Nature, who are wedded in that supreme symbol from tradition: Eliphas Levi's Baphomet, which is both ultimate woman and absolute man blended in a single symbol.

Satan is not a Christian invention. As Shaitan, he was invoked in Ancient Sumer; the Egyptians knew him as Set, and Had or Hadit; Hebrews called him ShTN, "Adversary". We

122

consider him to be a reality – *a reality in ourselves,* a reality of the animal mind, and the reservoir of the collective unconscious of humanity, stored deep within our genes, from all time. He is one-half of the human equation, the masculine, and is therefore naturally complemented by his other half, Babylon the Whore, the essence of the feminine from all time. Satan and Babalon, called by the Egyptians Hadit and Nuit, are eternally joined in their lust, and are the twin-sexed Baphomet, who was known to the Egyptians as Amen-Ra. Baphomet is simply the symbol of the union– the passionate lust between male and female – that is itself expressed, again symbolically, in Satan and Babylon. So it should be clear that these are not in any way objective entities, but they are keys that act in a certain fashion on the mind, and through the passion of ritual they empower the will and excite the consciousness to the point that it leads one to confront the full nature of oneself.

We are not a spiritual assemblage; we are a religious and psycho-evolutionary movement. Our ceremonial magic is simply self-transformative, not a lot of baseless superstition. We don't believe in reincarnation or any other afterlife doctrine: *we are immortal in our own time.* Also, we don't seek to convert others to our religion. If you aren't naturally one of us, from birth, then you simply aren't of us. Those who are naturally of us know it immediately upon hearing the glad word we preach.

Although we use Islamic-style imagery, we are not in any way Muslim – ours is a religion of Satanic Thelema. For us, there is no "light" and "dark" magic: there is but magic, and it works to ventilate our psyche through potent psychodramatic ritual, and to satisfy our love of dogma.

Whereas we don't believe in any distinctions in magic, we do believe that there are two distinct types of religion: that which classifies as white, a type consisting of all theistic or spiritually-based religions, and that which classifies as black, or self-based religion, in which the self contains, in its base unconscious, all the mind and power and glory of a God.

1. Our Lineage

Our Shi'a Thelemic Calendar begins with Year Zero, March 21, 1904 e.v., when with the writing of *The Book of the Law*, Aleister Crowley and Rose Kelly helped usher in the New Aeon of Satan, or as Crowley put it, "the world was destroyed by fire". We differ from orthodox Thelemites in a few ways. First and foremost, we believe that the rightful line of succession does not pass through Crowley at all, but goes instead through his most powerful Scarlet Woman, Leah Hirsig.

In 1921 e.v., Crowley, at his Abbey of Thelema in Sicily, swore an Oath of Absolute Obedience once and for all to his partner at the time, Leah Hirsig, who from that time on, according to our Shi'a

Thelemic tradition, received from him all power and authority both Satanic and Thelemic. As evidenced in *The Book of the Law* itself, Crowley had (and never transcended) his impudent ill will to the Satanic Law of Thelema, which is one reason both he and his followers, the orthodox Thelemites, denied then and continue to deny today, the Satanic reality of *The Book of the Law*. We Shi'a Thelemites do not follow Aleister Crowley and his worthless, slavish puppets; instead, we accept Aleisterion, a disciple of the line of Leah Hirsig. We are the first to fully expound *The Book of the Law*. We embrace Aiwaz, the name of that most ancient demon of Sumer, Shaitan, as Satan; and also unlike Crowley, we shed forever the decrepit dogmata of the Old Age of Gods, and wave the banner of atheism, knowing as we do that all supernal knowledge and power and wisdom abides not in any god, but in ourselves!

After Aleister Crowley abandoned the dedicated Hirsig, his life and career went steadily downhill. He became a slave to drugs, and grew increasingly destitute and scorned by society. Karl Germer, Crowley's representative in Germany, traveled to America after being released from a Nazi prison camp. Then in 1942 e.v., Crowley appointed him as his successor. Aleister Crowley died a penniless failure on December 1st, 1947 e.v.

Germer failed to initiate new members. He died in 1962 e.v., without naming a successor. It was not until 1969 that Grady McMurtry invoked his emergency authorization from Crowley and assumed the title of Caliph. In 1979 e.v., Crowley's magical order was reduced from a religious institution to a mere corporation. Grady McMurtry died in 1985 e.v. McMurtry, instead of naming a successor, requested that members of the Sovereign Sanctuary of the corporation elect one, which they did in 1985. William Breeze, or Hymenaeus Beta, was so elected, and he continues in the office of Caliph to this day.

Several different sects claim lineage to Aleister Crowley. Unlike all of these, we of the line of Alostrael (Leah Hirsig), do not claim lineage from Crowley at all: for we insist that the magical current that once drove Crowley on, abandoned him and his followers in favor of Leah's lineage.

Aleisterion went before the Thelemic community (those that follow the teaching, philosophy, and magical practice of Crowley), and made it clear that he believed he had magical lineage from the late Leah Hirsig, who however was purported to have died in 1951. He told them that he had obtained the conviction (primarily through a series of rituals performed in 1999-2000 --- December of '99 through January of 2000) that she did not die in 1951 e.v. as contended by biographers, but that she had in fact lived until 1975 e.v., long enough to have consecrated his mission. I, his partner, then befriended a member of Leah's family, and confirmed his conviction to be true.

Prior to her discovery, though, his claim was not well-met, and the contention that all the biographers were wrong about Hirsig met with mockery. Once word came from Hirsig's family, even the worst of his critics admitted that he was right.

2. The Book of the Law

The Book of the Law is the central sacred text of our religion, written by Crowley in cairo, Egypt, in the year 1904 e.v. It contains three chapters, each of which was written in an hour, beginning at noon, on April 8th through April 10th. Crowley claims that the author was an entity named Aiwaz or Aiwass, whom he later jealously coveted as his own "Secret Self". Yet his own words betray the lie: for he claimed that he had, in writing of *Liber Legis, The Book of the Law*, no right to claim any credit for the book whatsoever.

Its full title is *Liber AL vel Legis, sub figura CCXX, The Book of the Law, as delivered by XCIII=418 to DCLXVI*. Traditionally, it is abbreviated as *Liber Legis, Liber AL*, or *AL*. Yet originally, its title was given as *Liber L vel Legis*; and the book itself cautions Crowley (*but not others after him*) not to change so much as a single letter. It was his violation of this injunction, by changing the title of the book from *L* to *AL*, that was his most blatant and egregious error.

The actual title of this book, from the Shi'a Thelema point-of-view, is *Liber LA vel Legis, not Liber AL.* For whereas "Al" is the Hebrew for "God", "La" is Hebrew for "Not": and as we believe, there is no God. In fact, the book predicts that Crowley, being errant, would fail to fully understand its mysteries; but that one would follow after him, who would see it all clearly.

Crowley, inspired by that force of his own unconscious mind called Satan, wrote *The Book of the Law* on april 8, 9, and 10, between the hours of noon and 1:00 pm., in his hotel room in Cairo. The room was on the ground floor, and the place of invocation was the drawing room.

As he sat writing, the voice of Aiwaz came from over his left shoulder in the furthest corner of the room. It was a voice "of deep timbre, musical and expressive, its tones solemn, voluptuous, tender, fierce or aught else as suited the moods of the message. Not bass—perhaps a rich tenor or baritone." And it was lacking any "native or foreign accent".

Crowley was emphatic in his insistence that this was not a case of "automatic writing" or spiritualist "channeling", but that it was in fact an objective voice that had delivered the message. He admitted to the possibility that Aiwaz was a manifestation of his own subconscious, but he very much doubted that this was so:

"Of course I wrote them, ink on paper, in the material sense; but they are not My words, unless Aiwaz be taken to be no more than my subconscious self, or some part of it: in that case, my conscious self being ignorant of the Truth in the Book and hostile to most of the ethics and philosophy of the Book, Aiwaz is a severely suppressed part of me. Such a theory would further imply that I am, unknown to myself, possessed of all sorts of praeternatural knowledge and power."

Clearly, the mind behind the words was Crowley's own, but what isn't so clear is that this mind, this Aiwaz that was once worshipped as Shaitan, or Satan, was not merely Crowley, nor any demon or god or spirit, but rather, the underlying awareness of all men and women. Not just Crowley's mind, but the mind of all minds; this was, in short, not Crowley's book, but everyone's.

Crowley eventually got "inspired" (or so he believed) to write what he called *The Tunis Comment*, also known as *The Short Comment*. This served to seal the book forever from any expressed interpretation except for his own. He went on to write profusely about the book, throughout his literature and in commentaries. He became convinced that Liber Legis introduced a Law to regenerate the whole world, and that this book was to be the basis of a new religion.

But he died without providing solutions to the book's many mysteries and veiled cryptic puzzles. The book clearly predicts that Crowley himself would never do so, but that one would later arrive with those necessary answers. Yet with the shallow thinking of orthodox Thelemites, how is one chosen to expound it actually be listened to? According to these Crowleyites, it is "unlawful" to so much as discuss the book, and the Caliph encourages everyone to shun those that do so like the plague. It was similar thinking that led to the Inquisition.

The Tunis Comment cautions the reader against any expressed study of the book, and states that those who discuss its contents are to be avoided. The result is the idea that interpretation of this often cryptic book is an individual responsibility for each to decide on his or her own. However, some Thelemites simply ignore *The Tunis Comment* altogether, and do what they will: such are the fearless and the brave.

3. The Tunis Comment

Do what thou wilt shall be the whole of the Law.
The study of this Book is forbidden. It is wise to destroy this copy after the first reading.
Whosoever disregards this does so at his own risk and peril. These are most dire.
Those who discuss the contents of this Book are to be shunned by all, as centres of pestilence.

All questions of the Law are to be decided only
by appeal to my writings, each for himself.
There is no law beyond Do what thou wilt.
Love is the law, love under will.
The priest of the princes,
Ankh-f-n-Khonsu

We of Shi'a Thelema dismiss this comment as
uninspired and false, the product of Crowley's
imagination. And we go a step further, by
contending that, as we see it, the Aiwaz only
enjoined *Crowley* not to change the book, not those
after him. The last verse of the book states that the
book was "Written" yet "Concealed". It is our
contention that the book's key components were
veiled, couched in the obscure elements of Ancient
Egyptian mythology. We have restored the hidden
symbols in place of these "blinds", and have
revealed the book's true message in all its
unabashed glory, using the original, pre-copyright
manuscript of *The Book of the Law*, not the printed
version.

4. What is Shi'a Thelema?

Shī'a Thelema is a denomination of Satanic
religion distinct and separate from the orthodox,
spiritually-based Thelema of the Caliphate. We are
sympathetic to Aleisterion, the "child of the
Prophet", rather than the elected Caliph. Thus,
Shi'a Satanists consider the Scarlet line of

succession (i.e. from the Scarlet Woman Leah Hirsig, our patron Icon) as the true source of guidance while seeing the Caliphs as a mere historic accident.

Shi'a Thelema, like Thelema in general, is itself comprised of many branches; however, at this early time none is fully fleshed out. Unlike traditional Thelemic orthodoxy, however, we Shi'a Satanists are staunch individualists, not sheeplike followers of Crowley's rules. We impose no such doctrinal restrictions as you'll find in the more traditional camps (e.g. their superstitious and restrictive dogma that surrounds *The Tunis Comment*). In the Mosque, there is no degree system, though there are levels of involvement. Everyone is not equal; but nobody is your "boss" either. You must learn and accept our ways, and accept our ordinance (see below, *The Sevenfold Way* and *The Sixfold Ordinance*); but these are simply our own natural tendencies, not restrictions: *if our tendencies are contrary to your own, then you are not of us.* And though the Mosque shall most definitely accept donations from those willing and able to donate, you'll never be required to part with a single penny unless *you* want to.

"Shi'a" is the short form of the Arabic, meaning "the faction", in this case, the faction of Satan. It means simply, "members of the party", and it signifies the claim that Shi'a Satanists are the members of Satan, the symbol of animal glory, and they support in any way they can the Mosque of

Satan, His House, as well as the Prophet's true heirs which are the Shi'a Satanic Royalty that support His House. The true legacy of *Liber Legis* is with the revolutionary Shi'a of Shaitan.

5. Our Unholy Scriptures

We believe that we are the best source of knowledge about *The Book of the Law*, and the true Thelemic Royalty.

This difference between following either the Caliphate (Crowley and his line of descent) or the Scarlet Woman (and her line) shapes Shi'a Satanic and non-Shi'a Thelemic views on *The Book of the Law*; plus, we Shi'a Satanists have *The Black Hadith:* the first-ever fully developed Satanic system of religion built upon the Law of Thelema. And our commentaries on the Unholy Law, *The Satanic Commentaries*, are the only available complete commentaries in existence.

We do not worship Aleister Crowley. We do not admire or respect Crowley. We take from him what is ours by right, and dismiss him. Crowley violated New Aeon Law repeatedly, by abandoning his children (a severe offense in Shi'a Thelema), sacrificing animals (another egregious, Judeo-Christian-based error), violating his Supreme Oath to his Scarlet Woman and forsaking her, and by ultimately denying Satan (an idiocy since he referred to himself as "The Beast 666").

Not accepting the Caliph, the Shia recognize instead the religious authority of the Shi'a Satanic Masters and Mistresses that comprise the Elite of the Mosque of Satan.

Ours is the Shi'a doctrine of Thelema that the political and religious leadership of the Mosque of Satan is always to be headed by one from the Scarlet lineage of Hirsig.

The Thelemic Caliphate, on the other hand, maintains that Germer, the Caliph after the Prophet, did not appoint a successor to lead the Caliphate and guide the Thelemic community after his death, and that Grady McMurtry, one of Crowley's disciples, claimed the office of Caliph for his own. From their orthodox perspective, only *The Book of the Law* by itself, and Crowley's pathetic commentaries thereon (which are incomplete) remain the sole authority in matters of doctrine, while a Caliph is elected by consensus from amongst the community, whose authority is temporal and commercial, not truly magical. It is their doctrine that no further solution to the mysteries of *The Book of the Law* can ever come, except privately and without open discussion, each to his or her own individual understanding. This, to the Shi'a Satanist, leads to doctrinal confusion and magical anarchy, without hope of successful secular promulgation: who wants to devote themselves to a group that teaches nothing, publishes nothing new, and issues only century-old leftovers?

Shi'a Thelema, on the other hand, believes that servile humanity, consisting of those who are not of us, is there to serve us, the Kings of the Mosque of Satan, who are the lords of the earth. Shi'a Thelemites believe that all Caliphs, elected democratically or not, are usurpers of the Throne of the Beast.

6. The Sevenfold Way of Shi'a Thelema

1. Commitment. Dedication of one's life and effort to one's true will: to Our Lady Babalon (emblematic of undefiled love), to Our Lord Satan (emblematic of unrelenting will), and their concentration in oneself, Baphomet (Eliphas Levi's Two-in-One).

2. Ritual. Direction of one's life and effort towards improving oneself in all ways, and by using ritual magic to ventilate one's energies and receive the force of Satan.

3. Excess. Satisfaction of one's invoked energies in all kinds of activity, whether it be art, writing, work, devotion, playing, or all things joyous.

4. Vice. Indulgence in vices natural to us, however we desire.

5. Strength. Not mundane strength but strength of will to accomplish whatsoever we so desire.

6. Existentialism. There is no god, and we take responsibility for our lives. Our Satan is an impersonal part of ourselves residing deep inside the unconscious mind, a force or energy that cares nothing for us personally, but in which is to be found unlimited passion and joy.

7. Undefiled Love. We do not abase ourselves before the unworthy: our love is reserved for those that know the true meaning of love, those who are of us.

7. The Sixfold Ordinance of Shi'a Thelema

1. No Self-Loathing. Love oneself with utmost passion, joy, and delight!

2. No Fear. Fear not men, nor fates, nor gods, nor money, nor ridicule, nor any power in heaven or upon the earth or under the earth.

3. No Gullibility. We are sly, subtle, and sublime – not stupid.

4. No Harming Children or Animals. Animals and children are the closest living things to the nature and power of the Beast, and are to be loved and respected as we love and respect ourselves.

5. No Sacrifice. Sacrifice is a lie, for it is a denial of indulgence and a restriction on desire, and a contrivance of outworn belief.

6. No Abstinence. Sex is our joy and happiness, and a sacrament of the Beast.

8. The Fivefold Doctrine of Shi'a Thelema

1. There is no God.

2. There is no Fate, no Karma, no Destiny.

3. There is no infallibility.

4. There is no final authority among women or men.

5. There is no afterlife.

9. Shi'a Thelema in Practice

1. The Rituals. These comprise part one of our *Shi'a Thelemic Book of Satanic Ritual*, *The Black Hadith*, and consist of the backbone of Shi'a Thelemic

religion: rituals and ritual techniques to ventilate energies and acquire Satanic will to, if nothing else, enliven the soul and stimulate the dark, erotic corners of the mind. Our rituals aren't so tightly structured as to seem Catholic, quite to the contrary, they are designed to make good use of passionate emotion and ecstasy to wrap one's consciousness around The Infernal Snake. Most importantly, we use our own rituals, not those of Aleister Crowley.

2. The Feasts. Ceremonies for celebration of times significant to us comprise part two of *The Black Hadith;* like the rituals, they are loosely constructed to provide for the maximum of both enjoyment and effect on the mind. These are times of huge import for us, our chance to remember and honor great, iconic diabolists before us, and to celebrate great moments not just from history, but in our very own lives – birthdays, pubescence, weddings, funerals -- these are all events we celebrate with excessive indulgence. In some cases, as with solstices and equinoxes, it is a time to celebrate changes in our world. Whether it's feasts of the times or feasts to honor certain events in our lives, Sh'a Thelema religion is primarily Satanic in nature: i.e., the religious feasts celebrate us and our world, not some distant mythical god somebody invented!

Feast for the first night of the Prophet and his Bride: Remembering the union that brought us *The Book of the Law,* that of Aleister Crowley and the first Scarlet Woman, Rose Edith Kelly, we honor the day of their wedding, which was August

12, 1904. But as every man is an aspect of the Beast, and every woman the Whore of Whores, so too, in the Shi'a Thelema tradition, does this feast day also happen to be any given wedding or union of love soever.

Feast for the three days of the writing of the Book of the Law: April 8, 9, 10. We remember the events shortly following the Advent of Satan, in 1904 era vulgari, when *The Book of the Law* was written.

A feast for the "Ape of Thoth" (Leah Hirsig's nickname) and the child of the Prophet: This is to be the day of the "greater feast" (i.e. death) of the Child of the Prophet.

A feast for the Supreme Ritual, and a feast for the Equinox of the Gods: March 21, 1904 era vulgari, was the day of the Advent of Satan. We also celebrate the autumnal equinox and the solstices, as these are the times of great changes in our surrounding world.

Feast for fire and a feast for water; a feast for life and a greater feast for death: Pubescence in males (fire) and in females (water), is to be celebrated, as children grow into adulthood and start to know ecstasy. The "feast for life" is one's own birthday: the dawn of one's own divinity on earth: this is one of the most exciting feasts of all, second only, in the Shi'a branch of Satanic religion, to funerals, which celebrate life lived to its fullest. One's birth is known as one's "lesser feast", and

139

one's death is called the "greater feast". It is vital to note that we don't celebrate death more than life because we believe in life after death; rather, we celebrate because we realize that our brief but glorious moment in time is eternal in the memory of a life well-lived, for death though it is not a portal to other life, is nevertheless a joyous destination, when all life's joys collide in the consciousness at once, and transform that consciousness into purest ecstasy.

Feast every day in your hearts in the joy of my rapture: Each day is a day to rejoice in the unlimited joys of life.

Feast every night unto Babalon, and the pleasure of uttermost delight: Each night is occasion for ecstasy..

The feasts mentioned above are the ones all Thelemites recognize; but in the Satanic religion of Shi'a Thelema, we recognize the following ancient pagan holidays as well:

Candlemas: Feast day of Our Lady Babalon the Whore of Whores. February 2.

Hexennacht: Also known as Walpurgisnacht, this is the "Witch Night", the eve of Mayday, the Witches' Sabbath Night: a time of great revelry. April 30.

Mayday: Also known as Beltane. May 1.

Lammas: Feast of the harvest, by tradition; celebration of the culmination of Summer. August 1.

Halloween: Also known as Samhain. October 31.

Finally, we of the Mosque of Satan take care to honor certain events and occasions for their historical import. These are mainly lesser and/or greater feasts in honor of iconic diabolists of the past, as well as feasts to commemorate historical events of significance in the Kingdom of Darkness. Some of these are:

January 11: Since Leah Hirsig was so important an influence, being in fact the founding magical matron of the Mosque of Satan, we remember the day on which, in 1919 e.v., she took the Oath of the Scarlet Woman.

April 1: The date of the inauguration of the Abbey of Thelema, in Cefalu, Sicily, where Leah Hirsig eventually bound Aleister Crowley with the Supreme Oath of Absolute Obedience, assuming, from that point on, supreme authority in all matters Thelemic.

We do not celebrate the Prophet's lesser and greater feast days.

Finally, to us every day is a feast unto life, and every night a feast unto love!

Books and Mosque Materials

Our most significant book, our very foundation, is *The Book of the Law*, as translated and interpreted by us. There are two works we use: first, our version of *The Book of the Law*, which bears the title, *Liber LA vel Legis;* and second, *The Satanic Commentaries*, a complete elucidation of the mysteries of the book as we understand them to be.

Various Orders are presently being contemplated to operate under the Mosque banner. Each such Order will be designed to incorporate unique magical techniques to achieve their respective purposes. The members of the Mosque of Satan are subjected to no degree structure, and any magical work they do is their own choice, though we offer an extremely simple, but powerful, series of ritual guidelines and various routines to assist. The Mosque is comprised of three separate ranks: members, clergy, and Elites. Ordinary members have all the materials higher-ups have; nothing is secret. All members get access to the most important Mosque literature:

Liber LA vel Legis, The Book of the Law

The Satanic Commentaries

An Analysis of Liber Legis by Angloqabbalah

The Black Hadith (Shi'a Thelema Book of Satanic Ritual)

The Book of Satanic Magic

Debaucheries & Depravities (Black Sex Magic)

The Book of the Black Brotherhood (contains the 9ᵗʰ Hell Ritual, used by Aleisterion for various works within the Abyss; also, an account of unconscious exploration)

As of the time of this writing (Hexennacht, 2007 e.v.), the first three on the above list are complete. *The Satanic Commentaries,* however, will not be released until the autumnal equinox of this year. *The Black Hadith* will be issued this coming summer solstice. *The Book of Satanic Magic* will come out at the end of the year, for the winter solstice. *The Book of the Black Brotherhood* is scheduled for next Hexennacht. These are to be privately distributed as we have no publisher.

It is not disclosed how rank is awarded to members. Those who are given the rank of cleric are fully authorized to represent the Mosque publicly, and to interact with the public as they wish (if they so wish), to perform consecrations and weddings and funerals. They are expected to be perfect in their expression. Those awarded the rank of Elite have done a lot of self-transforming magical work, and have met with the approval of the Masters of the Mosque as full-fledged Black Brothers. Much of our system of magic, as earlier stated, is self-transformative in nature: it serves to promote accelerated evolution of the mind of the individual. Most of our workings and routines are solitary; but there are rituals for various group functions. The rituals and services are designed to be truly *fun to perform*, yet they constitute potent magic, with original elements and cunning psychodrama. The highest award, the rank of Elite, is totally secret and only awarded to a select number of individuals. Reception of this last rank reflects no actual attainment of any kind.

Satanas vobiscum!
-Aliana XCIII

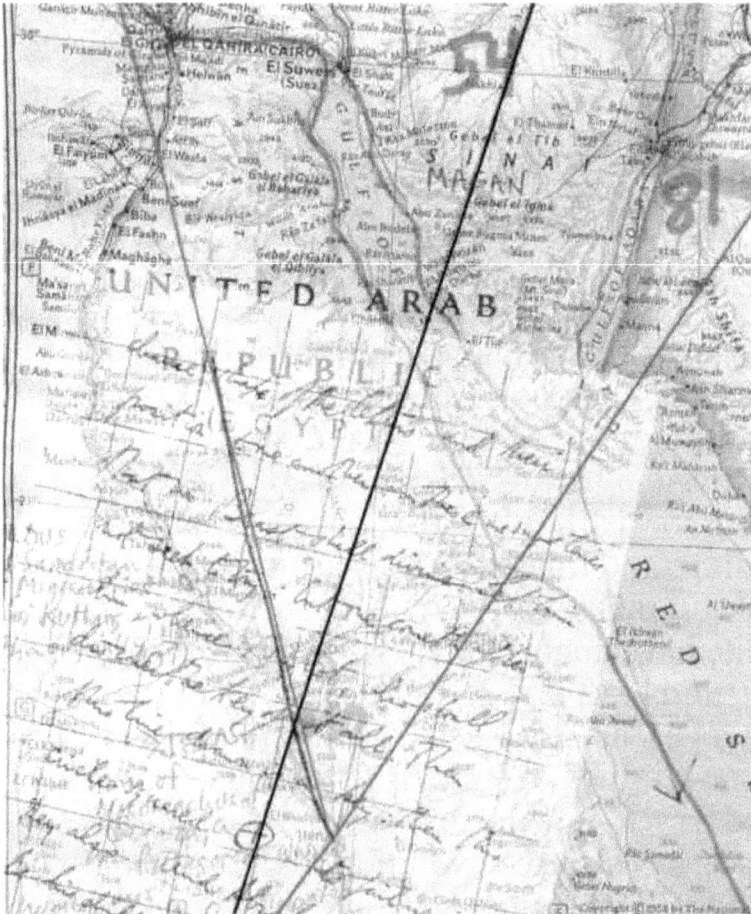

144

THE 93 VERSES OF GRIEVANCES AGAINST THE CALIPH

(with comments) by Frater Aleisterion

"Do what thou wilt shall be the whole of the Law." AL 1:40

1. In Nomine BABALON, restriction unto Choronzon, Amen.

2. To the second Caliph of Ordo Templi Orientis, in this 101st Year of the Aeon of Heru-ra-ha, in the interests of Liberty for the New Aeon.

3. First, there is the issue of justified exposition.

4. The prime canon of restriction is based on a lie borne of misunderstanding or else, it may be, deliberate self-interest.

5. That canon of restriction is THE TUNIS COMMENT, or THE SHORT COMMENT, of 1925 E.V.

6. THE SHORT COMMENT is a test of courage, issued from the Mind of Aiwass to weed out the weak from the strong & the brave; and also, to make known the demagogue who uses it to inspire fear through threats of expulsion in support of a restrictive interpretation thereof.

7. It asserts that it is forbidden to study THE BOOK OF THE LAW whatsoever, that it is wiser to destroy THE BOOK instead,

and it threatens any who disregard this injunction with direful peril.

8. It further states that those who discuss the contents of AL (THE BOOK OF THE LAW) must be shunned by all as "centres of pestilence".

9. But it finishes with "There is no law beyond Do what thou wilt."

10. You have suggested, with only superficial analysis of the dictum, in your Prolegomenon to the Second Edition of LIBER ALEPH, that Charles Stansfeld Jones, the first child of the Prophet, by commenting (as was his destiny and true will) on AL, might have wrought his own downfall, and that his was merely "one of the cautionary tales of the Path of the Wise".

11. Yet where is YOUR wisdom, Caliph of the Corporate Temple House of the East? for you seemingly fail to see the error of your logic, and proceed (in so doing) to tread upon the toes of the mighty Frater Achad, who opened his Eye upon the Key of the Law of Thelema.

12. And you do Achad yet additional injustice, by leaving the readers to assume that no more good came of him beyond his fall from the good grace of the Prophet.

13. You know full well, on the other hand, that Frater Achad only fell from grace before the eyes of the Prophet based wholly on a misunderstanding, that is, over the loss of books which the Prophet had assumed were stolen, which was a mistake.

14. You surely know, further, that Achad grew more lucent in his waning years, and expressed remarkable insights.

15. If therefore he fell at all, he most assuredly got back on his feet again, yet you give him no credit for this, for it supports your limited view regarding THE COMMENT.

16. The Voice of Aiwass, I assert, utters no contradiction without profound intent.

17. You have failed, in your fear, to pass its test of courage; and in so doing, you sever your tie (whatever it might have been, if ever it was, as testimony has you also denouncing lineages) to the Potency of Aiwass, whose Force & Fire cannot be withstood without virtue of courage.

18. There is, I offer, simple proof of my thesis with reference to THE TUNIS COMMENT, and it is this: AL states simply, in Chapter 1 Verses 54 and 55, that even the Prophet "shalt not behold all these
mysteries" of THE BOOK, but that the prophesied child would behold them.

19. Further, in Chapter 2 Verses 75 and 76, it is prophesied that this child would come after the Prophet and expound its riddle. Yet per your own restrictive enforcement of THE SHORT COMMENT, insisting that all who discuss the contents of AL be shunned, you restrict the very one (one of yet many to come) who is destined to assist in the understanding of THE BOOK's multitude of mysteries.

20. The Prophet said that "mystery is the enemy of truth", and yet you would keep AL's mysteries in the dark out of your failure to see THE TUNIS COMMENT for the test it is; and out of fear that you might lose hold to an upstart.

21. The Prophet also said that "fear is the forerunner of failure".

22. Your fear to lose control over the Estate of the Beast has driven you mad, or so it appears, for it spills over into your very policy, which AGAINST ALL THE WILL OF LIBERTY, has unlawfully removed LIBER AL VEL LEGIS, THE BOOK OF THE LAW, from the public domain where it rightfully belongs.

23. I assert my Right to print THE BOOK OF THE LAW as I will, seeing as that I perceive that it has yet to be published fully in accord with the instruction of AL Itself.

24. I assert my Right to quote from THE BOOK OF THE LAW as I will.

25. I assert my Right to expound THE BOOK OF THE LAW as it is demanded of me to do by that very BOOK Itself.

26. You, a mere Steward of the Estate of the Beast, have no right to deny me these Rights, by restricting me with copyright to that which it is unjust to bind, by this fact that it is mandated that one expound it.

27. Your fear is unwarranted, however, for if one truly expounds AL fully, and is accepted as this prophesied child, which is unlikely in your lifetime in any event, then your restrictions against him satisfy not the Law of Thelema, but only imperil your own agenda before all the Principalities and Powers of the New Aeon.

28. The office of child, in the New Aeon, is however one not of rulership but rather simple enlightenment, not to restrict any given view of THE BOOK OF THE LAW, but only to assist others to see additional truths otherwise locked within its more obscure Verses.

29. A child rules nothing, nor seeks to hold dominion over any part of the Estate of the Beast.

30. A child orders no one except in jest, but he always deserves to play as he will in the Light of the Vicegerent of the Sun, for none has any ownership over that Sun or Its Light.

31. Nor can a child harm any king, not even when mad at the same for trying to steal his Right to play in the Light.

32. For a child of the Aeon partakes only of the nature of Love, and knows nothing of the motives of greed.

33. This leads to the next issue, your seeming attempt to make a mere corporation of Thelema.

34. As I have cleared the air of the obscurity of THE TUNIS COMMENT, I may proceed with impunity to best explain what I perceive to be the basis of the problem, and thus better delineate my disputation in this matter.

35. AL enjoins the establishment of a clerk-house, which by your corporate policy I assume you think means to market the Temple.

36. Indeed, THE BOOK does say to do "well and with business way", but such is, I maintain, no business of any market, but the business of the Great Work.

37. For it is a fact that the word "clerk" has for its root the French "clerc" or "clergy".

38. It is no surprise, of course, that the Verse in which this injunction appears, Verse 41 of Chapter 3, follows immediately on the heels of that which portends: "But the work of the comment? That is easy..."

39. So easy, in fact, that a mere child can perceive it for the folly it is: for again, "There is no law beyond Do what thou wilt."

40. Because "There is no law beyond Do what thou wilt", you may do whatever you feel your will to be in this matter of marketing the Great Work, without any objection whatsoever; but whenever, in marketing the Great Work of the Beast, you strive to enforce restrictions of the market onto those Holy Books which are rightfully in the domain of all, you bind others in your greed.

41. Also for the images of the Beast: they are fully yours to protect, but in doing so, does it serve best to confine them, to limit their display by enforcing your right to display them exclusively?

42. This is for you to decide, as mundane law favors you, but is it right to horde sacred images?

43. Also for the symbols of Thelema: if they convey the Current of the Aeon, is it not better to share?

44. On these things I can make no demand, nor need I; but I for one am no profiteer.

45. If on the other hand my words turn someday, perchance, to gold, then I am obligated to turn gold into words, and thus propound even further the message of Thelema; for the word is all, and I am nothing but for the word.

46. Also, speaking of words, as "all words are sacred", no words can defile, therefore even if you disagree with mine, and I dispute yours, it is no right of either to interfere with those of the other.

47. So then, by this eminent logic, all factions at war should present their own Thelema their own way, with but fair warfare, and without any effort to subvert or repress the expression of the others.

48. All have the right to the Law, and free expression in the Law, no matter the dispute.

49. To deny this has its motivation in fear: the fear of becoming unpopular, and losing whatever value one has in the marketing of Thelema.

50. This brings me to my next grievance: the vilification, based in fear, of those who were sainted in Thelema and who gathered Thelemic honors before you.

51. The late Israel Regardie was one such; and what is your motive for casting him aside and seeking to erase from Thelemic memory the Great Work he did?

52. Indeed, he foresaw this, and he warned us that we might someday be robbed of his precious contribution to the legacy of the Beast.

53. And what was the reason he gave for this ill-treatment which he predicted? nothing more than uttering a few words of discussion on the contents of AL, and nothing less than having the courage to do so.

54. You cast out and insulted him; you threw away his excellent insights; you deemed worthless his wonderful wisdom and wit.

55. You did this, Caliph, to this great man who had helped the Prophet; and even though he suffered indignity from the Prophet, he returned near the end to further the work of the Prophet he loved.

56. And what expression of his so unnerved you, that you to this day help to bury his Thelemic contribution?

57. He dared, of course, comment on the matter of the child of the Prophet, extensively, in THE EYE IN THE TRIANGLE; and it was precisely this commentary that so inspired me, that without it, I would never be in this position at all.

58. Also, in his edition of LIBER LEGIS: he predicted it would be so.

59. Truly, we can see clear evidence of the foundations of your fear in your new edition of AL, which excludes much of the commentary of Crowley, particularly his references to other Beasts coming after him.

60. Clearly, those who have power are afraid of losing it; but there is no unlimited power in that to which you can cling.

61. You are afraid of a child.

62. But it is folly, and all the harm you cause to the memory of such giants that preceded you, is ill-advised; for again, you stand to gain for yourself only a little by not preserving the words of the wise with whom you might disagree, but in so doing Thelemic history loses infinitely more.

63. Yet it will not; and I only petition you, not out of dire need, but solely out of short-term
concern.

64. For if you ignore these grievances, it will avail you for a time, and I will be forgotten
for a time, but the momentum of those very Elders who push me on cannot but gain
Force & Fire with time.

65. And on my deathbed will the seal of the promise given in The Bartzabel Working be
fulfilled, then all will see the truth & be glad thereof.

66. There is, as it is Written, success.

67. And then it will be done with, this conflict brought about by closed minds; and as it
is also Written, so shall it be done: "Begone! ye mockers; even though ye laugh in my
honour ye shall laugh not long..."

68. If you would reform the Order, and address these grievances, there would be no
need to forsake you at all; but the Shroud of the Black Brotherhood clouds you, shutting
you up from the love of BABALON.

69. For this is evident: you permit no growth in the Order over which you preside in
your Osirian Way.

70. It is truly the Way of Osiris, this Dictatorship that dominates the Order of the

Eastern Temple; but Horus, on the other hand, proclaims: "Let the woman be girt with a
sword before me..."

71. Your Monarchy loudly proclaims: "Let there be no others before me!"

72. And that is no law.

73. Where is the New Aeon wine? it is as unplucked grapes on the vine.

74. What good is the bread, for those that are dead?

75. The Old Aeon is dead & done, but nothing is lost & nothing won; as it is Written, "all is ever as it was", yet we move on & on, and those of us who stand still shall get pushed on.

76. King against King? no, slave against slave, the Kings suffer no hurt at the hands of any slave.

77. But know this: we are all slaves & Kings; for it is Written in AL, regarding even the Priest of the Princes himself, in Verse 26 of Chapter 1: that he is the "slave of the beauteous one..."

78. There is here and There; and all is not here as it is There, but here & There are one, or as it is Said, They are none.

79. And none is holier than one; that is to say, BABALON stands before, not behind, the Beast.

80. Yet you seem to fear your women, too: for you make no reformation of the List of Thelemic Saints.

81. Fall not ill of the contagion that made the Prophet sick, for he was not only of the Old Aeon, he suffered further still from the hate instilled by his mother, who branded him Beast with no good intent, and so abused his mind that it wrought The Demon Crowley.

82. This was so the case, that he even turned his back when time came to honor his magical matron, by leaving even her, his forerunner, out of the List of Saints.

83. But our women are not ours, they are their own, and they demand no less than their share of remembrance for all they do, which is no less than all we do.

84. Reform the Order's weaknesses.

85. Abridge nothing of Thelemic history.

86. Rule with, not over, the women that stand proudly before you.
87. Revise the Rites of the Sanctuary of the Gnosis, in honor of OUR LADY BABALON and for the sanctity & virtue of the blood of Her Body.

88. Remove the mockers and do justice to Kings crossed.

89. I make with these grievances no demands, but I do offer wisdom, and you can take it or leave it, for I am certain it is no odds.

90. I reiterate: "There is no law beyond Do what thou wilt."

91. I shall do as I must do, and carry on this glad word.

92. For THE BOOK OF THE LAW is concealed no more, whether it be a little while or a long time before it can be made clear to all, it is no matter any longer.

93. Yea! Yea! the Law is to be Unveiled! & if it must sit in darkness for a while, that is your restriction on my expression of it; but at least I know that it is finished, and foresee its eventual manifestation.
It shall be Revealed. Witness My Seal: Aum. Ha. "Love is the law, love under will." AL 1:57 -Frater Aleisterion

COMMENTS:

A footnote should be appended to that last Verse. The reference is to Frater Achad, 1936 E.V., ADDITIONAL NOTES ON LIBER LEGIS, where he analyzes the word "Aum" and "Aum Ha": "AVM of Ch. I, verse 56, the seal of the "child," and which reappears again as the penultimate word of the whole Book Al -- Aum Ha." "Greed" = the overwhelming desire to possess. The true will is beyond such desire, but only seeks to indulge excessively for its own sake, not out of any drive or compulsion (irrational impulse) to control. A baby wants naturally, unlike a covetous adult that seeks control. "Business" = BUSY-NESS, essentially meaning, "do a lot of work and do it well".

THE BOOK OF THE LAW commands the child of the prophet to "expound it". Aiwass would hardly enjoin him to do so, then proceed to set a trap for him when he does. And "destroy this copy" is nonsense, unless one lacks courage, in which case it is probably better if one does so, considering that the psychological and magical forces invoked by THE BOOK OF THE LAW can be extremely difficult for weaker minds to deal with intensively. The TUNIS COMMENT is simply a test of courage. I assert my right to print THE BOOK OF THE LAW because it is my will to so do. I must do my will, and in time, my will be done in this matter. THE BOOK OF THE LAW, in AL 1:54-55, predicts that the prophet would not know all its mysteries, and then assures him that his child would. "Clerc" (Fr.) simply means "clergyman in charge of records and correspondence" (Collier's Dict.) The Old French "clergie", though, actually means "clerkship".

This is fascinating, because originally, as you can see by looking at the manuscript of AL, 3:41, the prophet wrote "clerkship", then inexplicably crossed out "ship" and penned "house" above it. There is no law, with direful repercussions, restricting the will to comment on AL, for Aiwass doesn't ambush the children of the Aeon in this way. I was told by Bill Heidrick that THE BOOK OF THE LAW is no longer in public domain and cannot be printed,

155

merely quoted to a limited extent. This places a restriction on what I can do, as no publisher will publish anything so bound. The prophet himself, it is to be noted, failed to profit much in his lifetime, in fact he only published at all, with no such success as he enjoys now, because he had an inheritance with which to do so. The Beast is lifted up, so will I be. Mockers, who cry aloud their folly that we mean nothing, will be shown for the liars that they are. The Caliph is interfering with me by chaining "his" Book with mundane copyright law. I assert, as I am Instructed, that he has no right to do so, and I stand opposed. "...the Law is for all..."
Aum Ha.

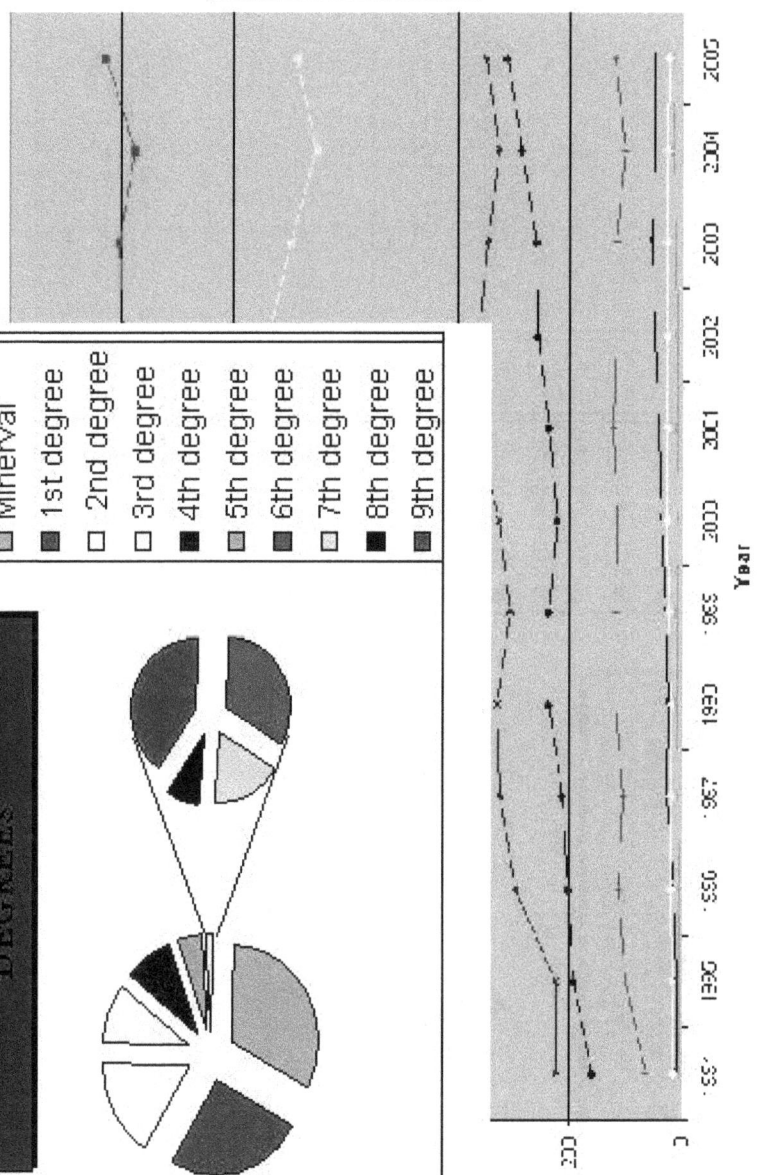

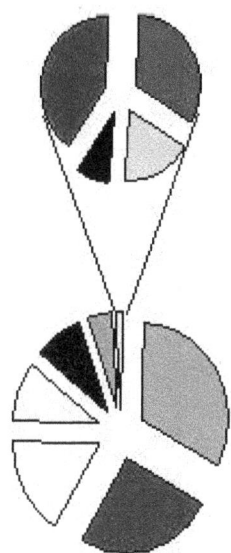

1994 OTO DEGREE -.6% NINTH DEGREES

Minerval
1st degree
2nd degree
3rd degree
4th degree
5th degree
6th degree
7th degree
8th degree
9th degree

2004 OTO DEGREE - .7% NINTH DEGREES

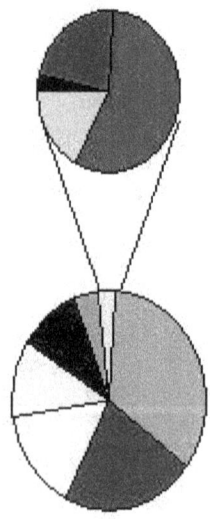

Minerval
1st degree
2nd degree
3rd degree
4th degree
5th degree
6th degree
7th degree
8th degree
9th degree

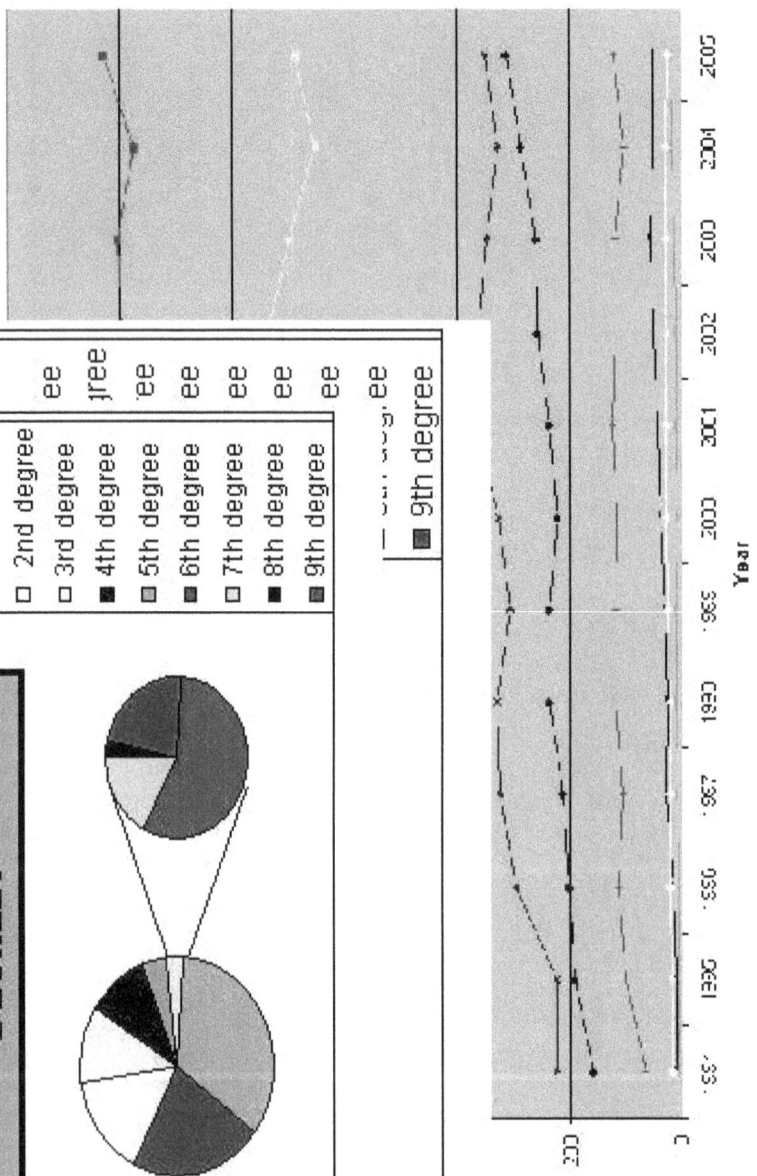

Israel Regardie's Revenge

If one were to wade through the psychic bogs of Golden Dawn karma, one in all certainty risks the danger of psychological and psychic damage, of losing impartiality, clear conscience, of electing sides in internecine psychic wars and political fighting in the Golden Dawn traditions of the late twentieth century and early twenty-first century. It is only with the armor of years of psychological therapy as suggested by Dr. Israel Regardie, in addition to trained mentors, life-long friends, peers, and our advisor Dr. Christopher S. Hyatt, years of Golden Dawn path working and initiation, Zen Buddhist meditation, and academic research into psychology that I undertake this venture into the Golden Dawn "flame wars" which have, at times, nearly set fire to the affairs of my friends and myself. My peers, and I (my close life friends) work under the aegis of the Cross and Rose, retaining its mysteries in our blood and pedigree.

Charles Cicero consecrated Isis-Urania Temple of a then independent, unaffiliated operative Golden Dawn research group in Columbus, Georgia in 1977. After much correspondence, Dr. Francis Israel Regardie traveled with Cris Monnastre in 1982 to Isis-Urania to initiate her and Adam Forrest (Lawrence Epperson) into the 5=6° Adeptus Minor of the R.R. et A.C. Francis consecrated the Vault of the Adepti at Isis-Urania, establishing the Second Order of the

R.R. et A.C. ensuring almost 100 years after its original charter the Lamp of the Golden Dawn continued in America.

In 1983 Dr. Regardie visited New Zealand, where a Stella Matutina lodge had been founded by Frater *Fenim Respice* (R. W. Felkin) in 1912 and continued to function. He accepted honorary initiation to the 6=5° Adeptus Major grade by Thoth-Hermes Temple headed by Pat and Chris Zalewski in Wellington, New Zealand. After his death, Francis posthumously received the 7=4° Adeptus Exemptus R.R. et A.C. degree by the Thoth-Hermes Temple in New Zealand.

Soror Cris Monnastre (P. Behman), who wrote an introduction in Regardie's *Golden Dawn* volume chartered with Frater Charles Cicero a new Hermetic Order of the Golden Dawn in Athens, Georgia with Regardie's other student Frater Adam Forrest (L. Epperson). According to my personal correspondences with Dr. Christopher S. Hyatt; he, Monnastre, and Forrest were the only individuals who received the 5::6 initiation and warrant from Regardie. Dr. Hyatt and Regardie chartered the *Hermetic Temple and Society of the Golden* Dawn, in addition to the *Israel Regardie Foundation*, and a "*Golden Dawn Research Society*" in Phoenix, Arizona in 1982. Dr. Hyatt took the fraternal motto, *Adonai Achad* in his Golden Dawn charters. Cicero, Monnastre, and Forrest's Golden Dawn organization was incorporated as a tax exempt corporation in the state of Florida in 1988.

Dr. Hyatt chartered another organization, the "*Thelemic Temple and Order of the Golden Dawn*" with David Cherubim in Los Angeles, California, in 1990. The organization simply was later called the Thelemic Golden Dawn and was a hybrid of Aleister Crowley's "Thelemic teachings" and a skeletal system of Cherubim's understanding of Golden Dawn material and alchemy. Cicero and Monnastre, whom was a former 'girlfriend,' and intimate with Regardie before he died in 1985, initiated David John Griffin, Frater *Lux Ex Septentrionis* into the Hermetic Order of the Golden Dawn, Inc. in Florida, 1992.

The Internecine Golden Dawn Psychic War had its roots in the personal contention between the Cicero's and Monnastre and Griffin. After Regardie passed away in Sedona, Arizona in 1985, Monnastre began dating Griffin on an intimate level. In January 1994, Monnastre, Praemonstratix General of HOGD, left the Cicero residence with Griffin after a personal argument according to witnesses.

Robert Zink chartered with his ex-spouse, the Eternal Golden Dawn which changed its name to the Hermetic Order of the Golden Dawn, Intl. (HOGDI) in 1993, renaming the organization Hermetic Order of the Morning Star, Inc. (HOMSI) in 1997, and again the Esoteric Order of the Golden Dawn in 2003. Monnastre and Griffin chartered the *Hermetic Order of the Golden Dawn/Rosicrucian A+O* currently a sole proprietorship under Griffin. Behman had operated the Hermetic Order of the Golden Dawn temples in Los Angeles throughout the 1980s.

After withdrawing her endorsement from that organization in 1994 to continue the unschismed version with Griffin, she eventually sold her partnership interest to Griffin in May, 1998. It is important to note that Monnastre's organization retained it the name Hermetic Order of the Golden Dawn, even referred to as the Authentic Golden Dawn by Griffin, until a trademark dispute was settled in 1996 when Griffin was legally obligated to adopt the appendent, "Rosicrucian A+O" to his Golden Dawn organization. Cicero and Forrest possibly had Monnastre "resign" from her Office and membership in the Hermetic Golden Dawn, Inc.

Monnastre separated herself from the company and association with Griffin's HOGD/A+O and sold her partnership interest to Griffin in May, 1998 leaving Griffin the sole proprietor of the organization. In February 1994, David Griffin charters the Isis-Nut temple in Stockholm and registers the Hermetic Order of the Golden Dawn trademark in Sweden. He immediately afterwards uses this trademark as the basis to register the same trademark in the newly created OHIM trademark office for the entire European Union.

Robert Zink, according to Dr. Hyatt who disclosed to myself the origins of this contention, fired the first shot in the Golden Dawn Psychic War by posting to Internet news groups online, private legal documents of Charles Cicero. Exponents of the Cicero Golden Dawn organization responded in kind by posting libelous accusations of a sexual nature against Zink also to online Internet news groups. In 1994, the flames began to spread to all corners of the Golden Dawn tradition, of which the smoke still smolders presently.

The maleficient libelous confrontations spread with the flames of a psychic warfare reminiscent of the schismatic, megalomaniacal behavior that fractured the original Golden Dawn. Various libelous "anonymous" Internet web sites and pages disappeared as quickly as uploaded to online servers, as attacks between Zink and Griffin infuriated Golden Dawn initiates in all organizations. In March 1995, Cicero filed with the USPTO registration for the Hermetic Order of the Golden Dawn trademark. Monnastre and Griffin hired Stuart Mackenzie, the attorney who won the Marcello Motta's Society O.T.O. vs. McMurtry's Caliphate Ordo Templi Orientis case to defend their interests and file formal opposition to Cicero's Golden Dawn trademark application.

Exponents of Griffin's organization accused Maria Babwasigh, Imperator of the Societas Rosicruciana in America, and Cicero of further libelous attacks. As backlash from the Cicero-Griffin trademark dispute, libelous and psychic maleficence against and from Griffin, Zink, and their respective sponsors increased in vehemence and quantity from 1994 to 1996.

In March 1996, March 1996 the Golden Dawn trademark conflict is settled temporarily. Cicero, Griffin, and Monnastre sign a legal settlement to share the "Hermetic Order of the Golden Dawn" trade name on a global scale. Cicero and the Hermetic Golden Dawn, Inc. is granted partial ownership of the mark in Europe. Griffin-Monnastre are granted the right to use the partial mark in the USA. At a 1997 International Golden Dawn Conference in the United Kingdom, Rosicrucian historian Dr. R.A. Gilbert delivers a lecture contending the history and reputation of the Societas Rosicruciana in America, an order that had been moribund owing to a legal dispute among senior members concerned with a breached real estate contract under former Imperatrix Lucia Grolsch. A new Imperatrix, Soror Maria (Babwasigh) took over the office and leadership of the S.R.I.A.

The *Rosicrucian Order of Alpha et Omega and its outer order the Hermetic Order of the Golden Dawn* proclaimed a *"Reformatio Fraternitatis,"* in March 1999, one hundred-eleven years after the original warrant of the Golden Dawn, moving all published Golden Dawn material to the outer order and replacing this material with a new Second Order curriculum derived entirely from confidential, pre-Golden Dawn Rosicrucian and Hermetic esoteric transmissions according to public announcements by Griffin. Chic Cicero, allegedly breaks his agreement with Griffin not to initiate each other's students by initiating HOGD/A+O member, "Mark Griggs." Griffin breaks off all business contact with Cicero. Griffin and his sponsors accuse the Ciceros of attempting to foment schism in the HOGD/A+O.

The Open Source Order of the Golden Dawn was founded by Frater Sam Webster in 2002 and based on a hybrid of Buddhist, Gnostic, Thelemic teachings, and ancient Egyptian theology. The organization grew out of a series of workshops on ceremonial magic held by Webster in 2001. As part of the 1997 Hermetic Golden Dawn, Inc. USPTO trademark principal register under the Ciceros, licenses were granted to the *Hermetic Sanctuary of Ma'at Order of the Golden Dawn*, *Open Source Order of the Golden Dawn*, *Sodalitas Rosae Crucis et Solis Alati*, and *Esoteric Order of the Golden Dawn*. {United States Patent and Trademark Office, Registration Number 2034866.} Cicero files a lawsuit in U.S. Federal Court against Griffin in 2005. Griffin's HOGD interests are represented by Florida attorney, Jorge Hevia III, whose fraternal motto is an unoriginal "D.eD.I.," a former member of Zink's Esoteric Order of the Golden Dawn who was expelled by E.O.G.D. administration.

More maleficient libel and psychic conflagrations appear in renewed defamatory posting on Internet forums and news groups in 2005 as a backlash to renewed litigation by the Ciceros against Griffin and the H.O.G.D./A+O. In February 2007, federal trademark litigation is dismissed with prejudice on both sides with equal basis. Not surprisingly, both parties to the confrontation swiftly declared victory. We conjecture that Griffin's attorneys led a 'scorched-earth' legal strategy, forcing the Ciceros to respond to nearly one hundred-fifteen filings, the majority of them frivolous. A "confidential settlement agreement" was reached that remains under the "perpetual jurisdiction or the court to enforce upon motion from either party on an equal basis."

Confidentiality provision of the Griffin-Cicero court settlement presently obscures a full disclosure of the relevant facts regarding the actual outcome of the case. It certain, that Griffin fully retains the right to call his order the "Hermetic Order of the Golden Dawn" adding the appendent "Outer Order of the Rosicrucian Order of the Alpha et Omega."

A renewed round of invectives rapidly circulate the Internet news groups and online forums directed by the usual suspects, sponsors of Griffin, Zink, and the Ciceros. In 2003, sponsors of Griffin's Golden Dawn organizations uncover invective Internet pages against Griffin, disclosed to have been published by Bryan W. Yronwode, Tyagi Nagasiva, or *Frater Nigris*, a Thelemic initiate of the Open Source Order of the Golden Dawn.

Griffin's sponsors uncover open letters by Zink and Joseph Max, Sam Webster, and Barbara Cormack, in an official capacity containing a diatribe giving explicit directions to one of these defamation sites published by Yronwode. Maleficence continues from all parties, and exponents of Griffin's, Cicero's, and Zink's Golden Dawn organizations rapidly appear and disappear on various Internet blogs, news groups, and forums until 2009.

Griffin and his sponsors in the H.O.G.D./A+O offered an end to the Golden Dawn Psychic War, offering a détente to Zink, Cicero and their affiliates. Griffin in his blog, proposed a "Golden Dawn Harmony Conclave" inviting all active members of all Golden Dawn organizations including the Adepti of the Hermetic Golden Dawn, Inc., O.S.O.G.D., and Zink's E.O.G.D. Expectantly, Griffin's offer is met with cynicism and suspicion. A détente appears to have held, as Griffin's H.O.G.D./A+O "Harmony Conclave" assembled on the Vernal Equinox in 2010, at Paris, France. The détente was short-lived, lasting until the Winter of 2010 when the invectives inevitably began once again and presently continue in 2011.

A root of the Internet and psychic confrontations between the Cicero-Zink-Griffin Golden Dawn and their exponents appears to be a deep-seated dispute about Golden Dawn initiation and lineage. Griffin and the *Hermetic Order of the Golden Dawn Outer Order of the Rosicrucian Order of the Alpha et Omega* argue that traditional Golden Dawn Initiation in physical temples is important and should not be abandoned, diverging from Regardie's and Cicero's view that self-initiation is effective as a psychological and spiritual tool in the outer order of the Golden Dawn. Cicero argues that traditional Golden Dawn initiation in a physical temple is not necessary in the grades and path-work of the lower Sefirot. Initiation ceremonies into the Sefirot grades of Malchut, Yesod, Hod, and Netzah, can be replaced by Self-Initiation. Cicero writes:

"Self-initiation into the G∴ D∴ current of magic has been a subject of much speculation and discussion. However very little practical information has been presented upon the subject. Israel Regardie was a vocal champion of the idea that a student could initiate him/herself through the grades of the Golden Dawn. He put forth the opinion that by repeated performance of such rituals as the Opening by Watchtower and the Middle Pillar Exercise, the aspiring magician could effectively be considered an initiate of the G∴ D∴ current. (Note: These rituals are provided in Chapter Six of this book.) However, he also stated that this hinged upon the student's own persistence, hard work and determination. The responsibility for spiritual progress is placed squarely on the shoulders of the student. There is only one person to blame if indolence keeps spiritual growth from occurring.
The need for Self-initiation is born out of the fact that it is not always possible for prospective students to live in an area that is close to an officially recognized initiatory temple. Especially here in the U.S., students have often had to spend a lot of money on transportation to an official temple in order to receive an initiation. Since there is a total of no less than seven initiation ceremonies required to become an Adeptus Minor, it is easy to see how expensive the process of traveling to a temple can become. This has led to various magical groups offering correspondence courses and astral initiation by proxy. However, these too are often highly expensive undertakings that do not address the solitary student's basic need to monitor his/her own psychic growth in a meaningful and spiritually fulfilling manner. (Some groups even bestow instant Adepthood with virtually no Outer Order training whatsoever; for a fee, almost anyone can get a certificate proclaiming one to be an Adeptus Minor [or even an Adeptus Exemptus!]. The spiritual value of grades obtained in such a manner is, of course, highly questionable.)" {Cicero, Charles. *Self Initiation into the Golden Dawn Tradition* Llewellyn St. Paul, MN 1998}

Zink disputes that traditional Golden Dawn initiation in physical temples is obsolete and has replaced it with Astral Initiation where initiates of the *Esoteric Order of the Golden*

Dawn are instructed to meditate while a ritual initiation is performed in proxy. I firmly agree with Regardie's insisting psychotherapy as a prerequisite for outer order grade work in the Golden Dawn. Dr. Regardie was of the opinion that self-initiation was practical in the Kabbalistic pathworkings in relation to the Tree of Life.

He felt that continual physical initiations below Tifaret, moving the psyche and body of light to Malchut, Yesod, Hod, and Netzach, created unnecessary psychic and psychological imbalances in the student and preceptors. The most critical initiations of the Golden Dawn occurred in the Neophyte 0=0 and Adeptus Minor 5=6 rituals. Regardie felt that the elemental initiations between Neophyte and Adeptus Minor left impressions on the psychic energy field of the initiate that simply mirrored the Opening by Watchtower ceremonies. (Regardie. *Ceremonial Magic*. Aquarian Press: 1982)

Self-initiation does not preclude the overall importance of physical ceremony at a lodge or temple; there are no self-initiation rites in Masonic lodges of any Rite or appendent body. The isolated student choosing to initiate independent of temple or lodge hierarchical dynamics must be as persistent and systematic as the hierarchical structure of their temple or lodge. Without consistent tutelage from proctors or formal temple officers, the self-initiating student must imbed the command symbols of each elemental initiation into their psyche and field of energy as a spiritual passport to be used in the realm of spirits. A self-initiating student, who has conducted the elemental initiations or Watchtower ceremonies repeatedly and progressively, embeds the same symbolism in their aura and energy field.

Including the Opening of the Watchtowers ceremony, the Middle Pillar ritual should be practiced and conducted repeatedly to amplify and reinforce the energy developed in self-initiation rites. The creativity and skill of the self-initiating student are also crucial to the outcome. Unresolved neuroses often rupture the personality and psyche during initiations and subsequent psychospiritual, and physiological modifications. These neuroses and psychosomatic blockages account for all the chaotic group megalomania in earlier esoteric fraternities and now modern occult organizations. Regardie recommended psychotherapy as a prerequisite for any magical operations including initiation. He refused to associate with any Golden Dawn temple that did not prescribe psychotherapy as part of its curriculum.

Unless these unresolved neuroses are therapeutically incorporated, identified, and allowed to emerge in consciousness in a safe and controlled fashion, operating with occult initiations allows neuroses to develop and acted out in dangerous patterns. Psychotherapy and initiation are similar in that both process unconscious patterns and integrate them safely into consciousness and prodigious methods of living and interacting with one's environment. The student who self-initiates into a formal system must learn to distinguish between organizations that instruct and educate, and personality cults. Many "occult orders," so-called, have their foundations around manipulative and charismatic personalities.

Addressing the need for psychotherapy as part of magical practice could have prevented much of the damage wrought by two major parties in the Golden Dawn Psychic & Internet hostilities. Since Robert Zink, David R. Griffin, and their respective accomplices revive internecine battles between competing Golden Dawn organizations, using the Internet as their battleground; we can easily deduce that both parties have an alternate agenda, both are keeping from the great Golden Dawn community. With each revival of the psychic and political hostilities by all parties involved, including Zink and Griffin's Golden Dawn groups, the Esoteric Order of the Golden Dawn, Griffin's H.O.G.D./A+O, and the Open Source Order of the Golden Dawn, their motives grow more evident.

Personal vendettas over litigations, and esoteric lineage disputes, e.g. group expulsions, counter-initations, valid charters & warrants, are clear in these hostilities. Money is a lesser-known agenda in the Zink-Griffin-Cicero hostilities. The 1995-1996, and renewed 2005 trademark litigations cost Griffin and the Ciceros a great deal, less money going to the production of Temple material, maintenance of Temples, and administrative functioning of respective Golden Dawn groups. Authors scrambled to pen and publish books attempting to counteract other Adept's new material on the market, and to help pay for expensive attorney's fees.

Griffin exhibits psychological obsession and potential neurosis with each response to Frater Zink's Internet postings on esoteric subject matter. With each Internet post, published Golden Dawn teaching, new website or blog, or any public statement by Zink, Griffin responds maliciously and systematically; rarely has each party produced new literature on the Golden Dawn teachings. A statistical search on Griffin's Golden Dawn websites, and related Internet sites turns up a clear and present obsession, and invective against his targets, rather than explanations and teachings of the Golden Dawn traditions.

When Regardie began to distance himself from operating Golden Dawn temples, and groups, as a trained Adept and psychologist, he must have observed the mass deterioration of stable Golden Dawn groups in the twilight of the 20th century. Amidst the chaotic personal and group diatribes, there are enduring Golden Dawn legacies established by Israel Regardie, operating under the Ciceros as the Hermetic Order of the Golden Dawn, Inc., the Golden Dawn Research Society, and its affiliated Hermetic Temple and Society of the Golden Dawn; both operated by the late

Dr. Christopher S. Hyatt; a life-long student and friend of Regardie. The Golden Dawn Research Trust is a co-operative of scholars and Adepts in the Golden Dawn tradition that publishes archaic rituals, lessons, and teachings of the Golden Dawn and Rosicrucian philosophy. The organization is based in Austin, Texas with an editorial team led by Darcy Kuntz.

The *Israel Regardie Foundation*^{TM} was founded originally by Israel Regardie and Dr. Hyatt in Phoenix, Arizona in 1982. Regardie and Hyatt established the organization to conserve the archives and Golden Dawn teachings of Israel Regardie in the form of published booklets, trade paperback books, and audio recordings. Falcon Press, now *"Original Falcon Publications,"* was the publishing house associated with the *Israel Regardie Foundation*^{TM}. In 2008, after the death of Dr. Hyatt, Soror Inanna and Joshua Seraphim reestablished the *Israel Regardie Foundation*^{TM} in an effort to preserve Dr. Hyatt's research collaborations with Regardie.

Dr. Hyatt's last days and passing saw the beginnings of litigation amidst his estate, splitting the old Falcon Press into two publishing houses virtually selling the same material. Joshua Seraphim retained several magical items, and unpublished materials given as a gift from Dr. Hyatt, including archives of emails, messages, and letters with the "Mad Doktor." The *Israel Regardie Foundation*^{TM} is an affiliate and subsidiary of Leilah Publications, Inc. based in Tempe, Arizona.

Intifádat

The virtue of mysticism and spirituality to the human condition is prevalent. The disposition of spirituality for the human species remains innate within our genome The motive of world religious traditions is that all men and women perceive to a certain degree, the everlasting wail of the Buddhist First Noble Truth, "that everything is sorrow," and religion consoles them by either an authoritative denial or perpetuation of this truth. This psychological ply is done via transgression of the situation itself, or by promising amends in other states of existence. A fundamental problem is that religions, without exception, often fail and become decrepit at the first tests of history and culture. The claim of religion is to excel, and incidentally, make obsolete the judgments of reason by reconciling mysticism and science. In this formula, a direct experience and more importantly expression of intelligences superior in kind to any incarnate human occur. Preconceptions of religion and the arts and sciences of the occult by the initiated scholar breed spiritual materialism and secular demonisation.

Esoteric religion presupposes ideals of a discarnate intelligence or experience of ultimate reality, regardless of whatever linguistic intrusion humanity places upon it. This is exactly what no religion has proven scientifically, trapping the human condition in its finitude and trance of sorrow. This is the great melancholy of Mankind, in which men such as

171

Marcus Aurelius, Schopenhauer, and Nietzsche have forfeited my definition of religion. Professor William James cites this melancholy as the abode of the "sick soul" (James, William *Varieties of Religious Experience* Modern Library 1999 pg. 52) where flesh and spirit lust contrary to one another in a state of all-encompassing schizophrenia. This spiritual schizophrenia is a healthy one that induces men, and women, to initiate into secret societies, religious fraternities, that since ancient times acted as custodians of highest cultural concepts and a depository of ordained knowledge.

Ceremonial initiations express a latent intolerable ache of the soul in Mankind to ameliorate this unbearable "sickness" by seeking a direct contact with the holy mysteries of God and religion. Theologian Emile Durkheim explains, "religion is a feeling of mystery." Durkheim states "*..all that is religious is the notion of the supernatural. By that is meant any order of things that goes beyond our understanding; the supernatural is the world of mystery, the unknowable, or the incomprehensible.*" (Durkheim, Emile *The Elementary Forms of Religious Life* Free Press 1995) Initiation invokes a sacred timeless theatre where the human drama of the romantic history of the soul is imitated, be it in the Cathedral, Temple, Synagogue, or Masonic Lodge, a pageant of initiation that is complete with tragedy, secret teachings, ordained knowledge, entry into Light, and the Mystery.

The use of the word *Islam* as a comprehensive term denoting he spiritual tradition originating from the teachings of Muhammad is a relatively modern development, emergent in Western society only in the last few centuries. In the 20th century, historical and private accounts over encountering Islamic cultures in Britain and European countries often used the now-rejected term "Mohammedanism." When Islamic culture was in its original ascendant within the Arabian peninsula, it was customary for its faithful to refer to the new spiritual tradition as a *din* ("religion"), to characterize it in

172

Quranic terms as *din Ibrahim* (the religion of Abraham) or *din al-Haqq* (the religion of the Truth, God's own religion).

The Arabic word *Islam* denotes "submission" (revealing a linguistic root with *salam*, "peace"), and was used originally to refer to the mystical features of Muhammad's *din*. The Hadith of Gabriel provides an effective exposition of the relationship between the experiential *Islam* and the general *din*. Umar Ibn Al-Khattab reports: One day when we were with God's Messenger, a man with very white clothing and very black hair came up to us. No mark of travel was visible on him, and none of us recognized him. Sitting down beside the Prophet, leaning his knees against his and placing his hands on his thighs, he said: *"Tell me, Muhammad, about Islam."* He replied: *"Islam means that you should testify that there is no god but God and that Muhammad is God's Messenger, that you should observe the prayer, pay the alms-tax, fast during Ramadan, and make the pilgrimage to the House if you are able to go there."* He said: "You have spoken the truth." We were surprised at his questioning him and then declaring that he spoke the truth. He said: *"Now tell me about Iman."* He replied: *"It means that you should believe in God, His angels, His books, His messengers, and the Last Day, and that you should believe in the decreeing both of good and evil."* Remarking that he had spoken the truth, he then said: *"Now tell me about Ihsan."* He replied: *"It means that you should worship God as though you see Him, for He sees you though you do not see Him."* He said: *"Now tell me about the Hour."* He replied: *"The one who is asked about it is no better informed than the one who is asking."* He said: *"Then tell me about its signs."* He replied: *"That a maid-servant should beget her mistress, and that you should see barefooted, naked, poor men and shepherds exalting themselves in buildings."* Umar says: He then went away, and after I had waited for a long time, the Prophet said to me: *"Do you know who the questioner was, Umar?"* I

173

replied: *"God and His Messenger know best."* He said: *"He was Gabriel who came to you to teach you your din."*

Umar's narrative is classified as an authentic hadith by Ulema (knowledgeable theologians), one of the most authoritative texts of Islam outside of the Quran itself. The appearance of Angel Gabriel to the Companions of the Prophet and the ritualized, catechetical exchange are distinctive in the revelation of Allah's imminence of judgment and revelation. The tripartite division of *din* into Islam, Iman, and Ihsan corresponds with the triad of degrees within Masonic and Rosicrucian initiation systems, and their modern occult derivatives. *Islam*, *Iman*, and *Ihsan* translated as "submission" (or observance), "faith," and "perfection" (or virtue). The three may be understood to correspond to the three "Blue Lodge degrees" of Freemasonry: 1° *Entered Apprentice* (observance), 2° *Fellowcraft* (faith), and 3° *Master Mason* (virtue). The initiation systems of the Societas Rosicruciana, and later the Hermetic Order of the Golden Dawn consisted of three "orders" with each degree denoting ascendant levels of esoteric philosophy and occultism. This triad of esoteric initiation and occult teaching was referred to by initiated members of these societies as the Man of Earth, the Lover, and the Hermit. The man of earth is the adherent. The Lover gives his life unto the Great Work among men and women. The hermit exists solitary, and gives only of their light unto men.

In Sufi doctrine, certain lineages, *tariqahs* ("chains," or "brotherhoods") to construe *Islam*, *Iman* and *Ihsan* as three points of psychic and spiritual evolution. The Muslim, the adherent who exercises *Islam* becomes oriented to *shariah*, which while it literally means "road," is ordinarily translated as "Law." The *Mu'min* (one who exercises *Iman*) embarks on *tariqah*, the mystical chain of spiritual enlightenment. And the *Muhsin*, adherent who exercises

174

Ihsan, acts from the state of *haqiqah*, the ultimate spiritual reality, where there is only contemplation with the divine.

Faith in God is unsurprisingly the first and foremost article of *Iman*. The *Din al-Muhammad* is the purest monotheism to emerge from the Abrahamic tradition, and it affirms God as consummate and distinct from the universe that is his creation. According to the *shahadah* or declaration of faith, God is one, an idea expressed in the theological concept of *tawhid* or unity. Sufi mystic teaching is a rich spiritual tradition that articulates Islam. From *suf* derives the term *tasawwuf*, literally to put on a woolen garment, figuratively implying an adherent to Sufism, or Islamic mysticism.

The balance between the exoteric and esoteric religious life for Muslims was not fully recognized in early Islam, giving rise to confusion by *Ulema*, the custodians of orthodoxy. The Holy Qur'an states that 'God is Light' and Sufism is an inherited tradition that identifies Light, *nur*, with Essence/Being, *wujud*. Sufi mystics like Ibn Arabi also spoke of the evanescence of Allah; Allah can never be truly seen and nothing may encompass Allah. For the orthodox Muslim, Allah is separate from *wujud*, contrasted with Darkness, *zulma*, Nothingness, as the cosmos is seen as an emanation of light between the two. Ibn Arabi teaches that His Eternal Position in the Divine Presence is in the World of Souls and Light. This is a timeless dimension. Allah brought into existence the pure darkness that is opposite this light, which is in the position of absolute non-existence opposite absolute existence. When He brought it into existence, that light flowed onto it with an essential out flowing with the help of nature.

Creation is the *barzakh*, connection, between light and darkness. Light, like Essence, is at once ontological and epistemological, associated with perception and knowledge. Sufi knowledge is a light that Allah throws into the hearts of men and women. This is the root of Ibn Arabi's mystical ontology, in that true knowledge is knowledge of the reality of Allah, a matter of opening and unveiling, *futuh al mukashafa*. The veils of existence are phenomenal causes and effects, or forms *suwar* that obscure the Light of the First Cause, of Allah's quintessence.

The Quran contains 99 sacred names of Allah, the "most beautiful names, *al asma'ullah al husna*. In the philosophy of Ibn Arabi, the names are a connection between Allah, his Essence, *Haqq,* and the created worlds. The mystical doctrines, such as dhikr (invocation) of Sufism shelter the heart of Islam. Mystical experiences are ineffable and the final authority to interpret the experience resides solely in the devotee whom experiences the realm of the sacred. The mystic in any religion is one whom penetrates into the mysteries and nature of the divine and the human condition.

The sufiyya are mystics, unaffiliated with interpreting the Qu'ran in a legal and theological manner. Due to extensive insights into the nature of the human condition, the Qu'ran, and Hadith, the Sufis were in essence the first psychologist of Islam, while the Ulema were the first legal scholars. Sufis sought to approach the human condition in Islam from an emotional, spiritual, and intuitive level, whereas the Ulema approach Islamic life on rational, logical, and theological levels.

Essentially, the Ulema can be considered exoteric whereas the practices of the Sufis, including the practice of dhikr and tasawwuf, are esoteric. El'Ghazālī sought to reconcile the two approaches to Islam, but it is debatable whether his success was limited. The Ulema and sufiyya offer intellectual alternatives to presenting Islam and its revelations to non-Muslims. The scholars of the Ulema are held in high academic standards to those whom would join their exclusive community. Ulema are the rationalists of

Islam, the legal administrators of the ummah, serving as guides. The sufiyya constitute ecclesiastical adherents to an inclusive approach to Islam that has enchanted non-Muslims. There exist within the practices of the Sufis sects such as the Aissawa and Naqshbandi Orders.

A theological divide such as that between the Ulema and the sufiyya exist in every religion, between the exoteric and orthodox, and the esoteric and mystical. The Ulema and sufiyya together have ensured the perpetuation and security of Islam as a religion. Without the scholarship and leadership of the Ulema, Islam could not have secured itself from exterior assimilation and dysfunction. Without the sufiyya, there would already exist in Islam the capacity for self-renewal and enlightenment, and Islam would, in my opinion, lack the livelihood of the revelation of the Qu'ran and become a tomb rather than a vehicle of human spiritual elevation.

Sufism is a mystical teaching, a Freemasonry whose true origins lay not in the Qur'an or the *Din al-Muhammad*, the true origins of Sufism remain with the Invisible College, never traced or dated. Sufism, like Freemasonry is at home in all religions; as Free and Accepted Masons lay before them in their Lodges a sacred book of choice - Bible, Qur'an, Torah, all religion is accepted as a temporal state. If Sufism shelters the heart of Islam, this is because Sufism is the secret teaching of all ages, within all religions. Sufi, like "Quaker," is just a moniker. Mystic poets were the chief disseminators of Sufi thought. Sufis have always insisted on practical spirituality. Metaphysics are of no use without practical illustrations of prudence that nothing can intoxicate save union with the divine; these poetic illustrations are supplied by popular legends, music, and fables.

Sufism is revealed in the world by means of itself, while occultism in the United States and Europe is revealed by means of progressive initiations, yet in the 21st century there is no longer any such thing as "occultism" in the United

States, or Europe. Surrounded by modes of digital exposure
on a global scale, Sufism retains its mystic quality without
Internet dissemination. Sufism is the grand demarcation
between the human subconscious mind and religion. Where
American occultism is concerned with the pursuit and
collection of hidden teachings and the engineering of
consciousness, Sufism's concern is for the freedom of ideas,
an intolerance against cruelty, hypocrisy, and religious
persecution; their opposition was to injustice and political
crime. Their stories were the subject of divine intoxication,
love, and human suffering.

Sufi mystical poetry is the biography of humanity.
Their poetry defies fortune and outlives the world's
calamities. They are an eternal edifice surviving all empires,
conquerors, kings and revolutions. Sufism is a comfort to the
broken heart, immortalizing the poet, consoling the mind's
silent tragedies. These are the courageous souls who paint
visions of apocalypse and ecstasy across the night skies.
Sufism is the Arabic parent of Freemasonry, the true "Eastern
Star" of the Western Mystery Schools. The Arabic word for
Mason, is *al'Banna*, "builder." The fundamental word for the
Royal Arch School of Masonry, is *Jahbulon*, composed
usually of the Hebrew letters, Aleph, Beth, and Lamed - A, B,
and L. According to The Rev. Canon Richard Tydeman, in
an address to the Supreme Grand Chapter of England on 13
November 1985, the word is a compound of three Hebrew
terms: יה *Jah*, I AM, which indicates eternal existence, בעל
B'El, on high, in heaven) and און*On*, strength; pronouncing
three aspects or qualities of Deity, namely Eternal Existence,
Transcendence, and Omnipotence and equating to The True
and Living God.

According to Stephen Knight, following Walton
Hannah, the word is a compound of the names of three gods
worshipped in the ancient Middle East: Yahweh/Ja, Baal, and
On, a name in Genesis in the Bible in Potiphar priest of On;

thought in older times to be a name of Osiris. The letters A, B, and L represent the Sufi watchword *al'Banna*. To the Sufi builders, the word intimates initiation and the three letters symbolize key meditation postures. A, *alif*, is the kneeling posture. The second letter, B, *ba*, is symbolic of prostration and concentration. The third letter, L, *lam* in Arabic is shaped like a rope. To the builder, lam means 'the rope which binds all in mediation.'

The letters *alif*, *ba*, and *lam* according to the mystic Abjad table when added together produce the sum of 33. *Alif* ا = 1, *ba* ب = 2, and *lam* ل = 30. According to the Sufi builders, this code is an intimation of the letter Q, the Masonic letter 'G,' inscribed by the builders with a pentagram. In the Golden Dawn and other Hermetic traditions including Rosicrucian philosophy, the superimposed triangles represent male and female, fire and water, solve et coagula. The lower triangle correlates to the shaped Arabic numeral seven, the upper is the outline of the numeral eight, with the sides of the triangles comprising the sum of six. The series 786 is the esoteric code of *Bismillah ar-Rahman ar-Rahim* reduced by direct substitution in the Abjad. The phrase means In the name of *Allah the Beneficent, the Merciful.*

The term "old religion" is what the ancient pagan peoples of Europe referred to their folklore and spiritual ancestral rites; the Druids, Celts, Norse, Aryans all possess arcane esoteric traditions steeped in history's twilight. Sharing the same shadow is the antique faith of the Sufi and Arabian traditions. It is stressed in the *ghazalis (mystic love poems)* of Hafiz, Rumi, Ibn El'Arabi and the great Sufi mystics. Wandering Sufis contributed to the esoteric origins of the old faith of witchcraft in Europe. According to Sufi historian Idries Shah, a cult of dancers and poets called the *Maskara* used a ritual form of whirling dance, and ceremonially infused a liquid form of the hallucinogenic plant, *datura*. The Maskara were said to be founded by the potter and renowned mystic poet, *Abu el-Arabiya*   . Atahiyya's collection of mystical ghazals was commemorated by his Moorish Sufi disciples in 9th century Spain.

The Maskara were called the "Revelers" by European pagans of the old mystery religions. Their influence is found in the Spanish word for witch, *'brujah'* a linguistic evolution of *mabrush* a Maskara word meaning *"intoxicated by the thorn apple* (datura.)" Atahiyya's circle of Sufi Bedouins signified his tribe with the name *Anz, Aniza* with a torch between the horns of a goat head symbolizing for the Anizas the light of illumination from the intelligence (head). His *wasm*, a tribal branding, customary for Bedouins, resembled a broad arrow and was called an eagle's foot. Moorish witches in Spain called the Maskara symbol, a 'goosefoot' that was often used to mark coven meeting groves in secret.

The Hashish Takers, as referred to by Farhad Daftary and Dr. Bernard Lewis, are known commonly as the Order of Assassins, and according to scholars initiated a political and economic connection with the Templar Order. Templars often employed Arabic secretaries in the eastern chapters, as many Knights were fluent in Arabic. The Templars were exposed to many ritual customs the Roman Catholic ecclesia were not ordinarily exposed to. In 1308, one-hundred and twenty-seven articles of accusation were read aloud against the Templars, the major theme of the malediction being idolatry, and debauchery. The Templars were accused of idolizing the *Maskara* goat's head with the illuminating flame between the two horns of fertility. The goat's head was called Baphomet, or *Bafomet*, by Roman Catholic inquisitors. Western scholars like Daftary and Lewis suppose that the term Bafomet has no connection with Muhammad, or Mahomet. Bafomet is more likely a corruption of the Sufi *abu-fihamat*, 'head of wisdom," in Sufi terminology, *ras el-fahmat* translates to "head of knowledge," esoterically meaning the mutation of man's intellect after initiation; the transmuted consciousness of the *futuh al mukashafa.*

"Knowledge, and Understanding" in Sufi terminology derives from the Arabic root, 'FHM.' FHM is a derivative from Fehm, "wisdom," also a connotation of "black," "or coal." The theme of the goat's head used by the Templars and Sufi mystics resurfaces repeatedly in the history of the Invisible College and its derivative mystery schools. Surah 24 *An-Nur* of the Qur'an illuminates the heart of Sufi mysticism. The verse *An-Nur* means "The Light," expounds on the nature of *nur*, with Essence/Being, *wujud* the evanescence of the dimensions of human consciousness outside of intellect and emotion. *Nur* can never be truly seen and nothing may encompass it, contrasted with Darkness, *zulma*, Nothingness, as the cosmos is seen as an emanation of light between the *Allah* and *Zulma*. Surah 24 *An-Nur* teaches that our Eternal Position in the Divine Presence is in the World of Souls and Light.

Compare Surah 24 (verse 35) *An-Nur: "ALLAH is the reflection the Light to the heavens and earth. His Light resembles a lamp within a niche. The lamp is enclosed in a crystal, like a brilliant star. Lit from a blessed tree, an olive, not of the East or the West; of it the oil is well nigh-luminous, though the sacred fire touches it, Light upon Light!"* and Surah 86 *El Tariq,* (verse 1-4) the Night Visitant: *"In the name of God, most benevolent, ever-merciful...How will you comprehend what the night star is? It is the star that shines with a piercing brightness... That over each soul there is a guardian."* Nature and life are a conundrum; we are here to make out the mysteries of life and death and draw them into the Light. Sufi mystics are the guardians of secret teachings of all ages obscured by an underculture of living shadows determined to find the antique faith in plain sight.

Qutub in Sufi terminology refer to the reputed invisible heads of all Sufis, of all Sufi tariqas and lineal chains. The word means, "pivot, chief, pole" transfigured to

181

the sum 111 with the Abjad table. Qutbuddin are guides on earth who know the secret powers of the heart could reprogram their minds and psyche at will, and can unlock the underlying secrets of human psychology. Qutbuddin are the conquerors of hearts, the lords of annihilation represented by black robes frequently worn by dervishes and Sufi masters. Qutb in Sufism is the perfect human being, *al-insān al-kāmil*, a "pole" leading all Sufis and all men. There are said to be only five Qutbuddin living at once in any period of history.

The knowledge and possession of secret religious formulas is necessary for the station of *qutubiyyah*, the mystic state of perfection of a Sufi Qutb. *Qutubiyyah* correlates to the Christian mystic state of Gnosis, or saintly beatification. The transcendent reality taught by the Sufis and the Prophet Muhammad, Arabic - *al-ḥaqīqa al-muḥammadiyya* resembles the sun, and the hearts of the Qutbuddin are moons reflecting the permanent light of Allah. According to many Sufis, the elite stage of mysticism for Qutbuddin beings at the end of the point of spiritual prophethood. The end of the prophets therefore would be the starting point for the spiritual elite, the Qutbuddin, or "illuminated ones."

The *Qutb* is the axis or pivot and the highest station in the Sufi hierarchy. Qutbuddin are directly responsible for the welfare of the entire world. Qutbuddin are said to be the spiritual successor of Prophet Muhammad. All Sufis are in essence, reflections of Qutbuddin; they believe in the integrity of the human race. Sufis urge the existential self to attain an organic union with the human species and with the meta-physical ground of the cosmos. Sufis value life, personality, art, and transcendent love. Sufis do not claim their teachings as a religion or even a law of human social development. Sufism is an uprising, an intifada, and reinstatement of the human species' latent spiritual and intellectual impulses under the aegis of universal philosophy.

Sufi mystic poets in their verses show us that no
religion has a monopoly over truth. That Sufism is the
antique faith offering the relief of human misery and spiritual
evanescence. For a Sufi, the World of Souls and Light is the
point where life starts and where it ends. Tracing its earliest
theology to the lifetime of Muḥammad, the mystic sect of
Nizari Ismā'īlism rose to become the most influential branch
of Shī'ism, climaxing as a political power with the Fatimid
Caliphate in the tenth through twelfth centuries. Nizari
Ismā'īlīyya get their name from their acceptance of *Ismā'īl
ibn Ja'far* as appointed spiritual successor, *Imām*, to *Ja'far
aṣ-Ṣādiq*, herein they differ from the Twelvers, who
distinguish *Mūsà al-Kāẓim*, younger brother of *Ismā'īl*, as
true Imām.

Hassan Ibn Sabbāh was a Persian mystic raised as a
missionary and took his early education in Qumm, Persia. At
the age of 17, Hassan converted to Nizari Ismā'īlism and
swore allegiance to the Fatimid Caliphate in Cairo, Egypt.
He continued his studies there for three years then traveled to
Palestine, Syria, Azerbaijan, and Turkey after becoming a full
missionary, or *Dā'ī*. Hassan's search for a base from where
to guide his mission ended when he located the castle of
Alamut (Arabic; *Aluh Amut* "Eagle's teaching") in the Rudbar
area of northern Persia in 1088. In the summer of 1090[AD],
Hasan set out from Qazvin to Alamut on a mountainous route
through Andej. He remained at Andej disguised as a
schoolteacher named *Dikhhuda* until he was certain that a
number of his supporters had strategically positioned below
the castle in the village of Gazorkhan and had gained paid
labor as scribes and tutors at the fortress itself.

During the early weeks of the month Rajab of Year
483 of the Islamic Hijri calendar, Sabbāh and around 30-40 of
his loyal *hashishi* declared complete control of the fortress
Alamut. Historians record that Sabbāh's band of hashishi
swore their lives to his new teaching on the 14th day of Rajab

183

establishing the first oaths of the *Hashishiyya*. (Virani, Shafique N. *"Ismailis in the Middle Ages: A History of Survival, A Search for Salvation"* (New York: Oxford University Press, 2007), 29.)
It was September 11, 1090.

Hassan's takeover of the fort was one of silent surrender in the face of defeated odds. To affect this takeover Hassan employed an ingenious strategy: it took the better part of two years to effect. First Hassan sent his *Da'iyyīn* and *Rafīks* (missionaries and foot soldiers) to entice the villages in the valley over through propaganda. Next, key Ulema were converted and by the end of 1090, Hassan took over the fort, establishing a base for his theology and political exploits. Hasan bin Sabbāh compiled a theological treatise in this context, entitled *Fusul-i Arba'a*, "The Four Chapters," which was an *Ismā'īli* thesis, and the doctrine of *talim* was expounded by him in this Persian tract.

The *Hashishi* of the *Nizari Ismā'īliyya* sect caught the attention of Crusaders and Medieval historians with the increase in their political assassinations. Medieval historians designated the Hashishi pejoratively as *Batiniyya* (esotericists, or sorcerers), or *Ta'limiyya*, sometimes Nizāriyyah. Hashishi, like all *Nizari Ismā'īliyya* were designated *malahida*, or *mulhiddun*; derogatory terms meaning "heretics." The terms *al-Hashishiyya* (the hashish users), and *Jama'at al-Hashishiyya* (community of the hashish takers) were meant to be abusive and belittling by anti-Nizari polemical edicts, or fatwas, issued by the Fatimid chancery around 1123[A.D.] on behalf of the Caliph. This anti-Nizari condemnation of *Hashishiyya* stemmed from Sunni theological disapproval and the growing political crisis of the First Crusades.

These abusive terms first applied to the Syrian Hashishi in the early decades of the twelfth century, indicating a general familiarity with the sect in Syria and Egypt. Many of the terms were used interchangeably by orthodox Sunni Imams. Hashishi is not used by Persian historians Rashid al-Din, and Juwayni of the Nizari period, who are the main sources of information on the sect in the Fatimid Caliphate. Muslim historian Ibn Khaldun uses the term *Fidawiyya* (zealots), in reference to al-Hashishi writing after the thirteenth century. Based on historical references the Hashishi were rarely referred to as "hashishi takers" until decades after Hasan bin Sabbāh.

Hashish use in Syria, Egypt, and Persia grew extensively by lower social strata. Muslim scholars wrote numerous tracts on the effects of hashish use in various physical, mental, ethical, and religious considerations. Hashish users were commonly considered social outcasts and religious heretics. The few Islamic historians that refer to the Nizaris as Hashishiyya, like Juwayni, never explain the reasons for this label in terms of hashish use, though heaping libelous accusations upon the sect that enabled exotic fantasies by Medieval European historians such as Marco Polo.

One need not be a religious studies scholar, or even an initiate into the Mystery Schools to realize that Sufi and Islamic contributions to the arts and sciences, to human spiritual development are immense. Our culture owes a great debt in cultural development to Sufism and Islamic mystical societies. A synchronicity of initiation from ancient Ægyptian mortuary rites to secret bacchanalia of Mithraic temples and ceremonies of the Scottish and York Rites have become the axis of the one true antique faith. All of Sufism is synchronous with the religions of the world. Occultism has remained a shifting undercurrent for nameless magic bequeathed to an Invisible College. The strength of the one true antique faith lies in concealment, never appearing throughout history in its own name, always veiled upon veils by other names and institutions.

The teachings of Sufism orchestrate throughout history within secret societies, traced in pedigree and language with syncretism. In the Twenty-first century, Christianity, Judaism, and Islam all share a fragile precarious world stage, leading societies teasingly close to economic and social ruin in the name of faith and "liberty and equality," the opiate of religions. Consider the antique faith of Sufism, Masonic, and Rosy Cross fraternities that are tagged as conspiratorial networks, determined to establish a "new world order." Sufi societies contribute and engage in humanitarian endowments of education, scholarship, chivalry, and public service for a greater good ignored by a cadre of conspiracy racketeers.

Orthodox Islam, both Sunni and Shi'a generally prohibit the practice of Freemasonry, and forbid Muslims to join Masonic Lodges in Arab nations with a sharī'ah legal system, An influential body interpreting Islamic Law correlating interfaith dialogue is the Islamic Jurisdictional College. At its meeting on 15 July 1978, it issued an opinion concerning *"The Freemasons' Organization."* The IJC declared: *"After complete research concerning this organization, based on written accounts from many sources, we have determined that:*

Freemasonry is a clandestine organization, which conceals or reveals its system, depending on the circumstances. Its actual principles are hidden from members, except for chosen members of its higher degrees.

The members of the organization, worldwide, are drawn from men without preference for their religion, faith or sect.

The organization attracts members based on providing personal benefits. It traps men into being politically active, and its aims are unjust.

New members participate in ceremonies of different names and symbols, and are frightened from disobeying its regulations and orders.

186

Members are free to practice their religion, but only members who are atheists are promoted to its higher degrees, based on how much they are willing to serve its dangerous principles and plans.

It is a political organization. It has served all revolutions, military and political transformations. In all dangerous changes, a relation to this organization appears either exposed or veiled.

It is a Jewish Organization in its roots. Its secret higher international administrative board are Jews and it promotes Zionist activities.

Its primary objectives are the distraction of all religions and it distracts Muslims from Islam.

It tries to recruit influential financial, political, social, or scientific people to utilize them. It does not consider applicants it cannot utilize. It recruits kings, prime ministers, high government officials and similar individuals.

It has branches under different names as a camouflage, so people cannot trace its activities, especially if the name of "Freemasonry" has opposition. These hidden branches are known as Lions, Rotary and others. They have wicked principles that completely contradict the rules of Islam. There is a clear relationship between Freemasonry, Judaism and International Zionism. It has controlled the activities of high Arab officials in the Palestinian problem. It has limited their duties, obligations and activities for the benefit of Judaism and International Zionism."

After the destruction of Alamut by Mongol King Hulegu in 1256, adherents of the Nizari Ismāʿīliyya sect fled to Afghanistan, the Himalayas and Kashmir. Fleeing the Mongol hordes, the Nizaris had migrated to India as early as the eleventh century, but the founder of the branch of the sect

187

known as the Bohras, one Abdullah traveled from the Yemen arriving in Cambay, India around 1067. He traveled and taught extensively in the kingdom of Gujarat, where currently the Bohras actively a secretive presence, practicing Ismāʿīlism.

The other major branch of the Nizari Ismāʿīliyya in the East today are known as the Khojas, who are particularly strong in what was once the Punjab but is now part of Pakistan. Khoja tradition relates that a da'i known as Nur Satagut, literally 'teacher of true light,' was the first to arrive in India. Satagut traveled to Punjab India between 1160 and 1242[A.D.] The Khoja sect that descended directly from the Nizari Ismāʿīliyya Hashishi, Assassins, and the Aga Khan's leadership of the Ismāʿīliyya is based today on their support.

The current Aga Khan, correctly recognized as Prince Karim El Husseini, Aga Khan IV, is recognized as the forty-ninth hereditary imam of the Ismāʿīliyya claiming direct descent from the Prophet Mohammed and the Nizari Hashishi. He is recognized as head of the world-wide Ismāʿīliyya sect, today estimated at between four and twenty million in number. A 1985 estimate by theologians lists Aga Khan IV's income from voluntary contributions at seventy-five million British pounds a year.

The theological stratagem of the revolutionary genius Hassan Ibn Sabbāh is the first indication of a religious and political Persian ethos after the conquest of the country of the Arabs and consequent conversion to Islam. In a broad sense, the philosophy and military tactics of the Hashishi undoubtedly had an enduring influence in the religious and political life of Islamic development in the Middle East and resistance to colonial imperialism. Hashishi legacy is shared by both the Aga Khans and by contemporary "Arab spring" revolutionaries in Egypt, Syria, Tunisia, Yemen, Libya, and other Arab countries resisting decades of state-sponsored oligarchy.

Beginning in the 1820's, a group of da'is (missionaries) were appointed by a combined movement of Oxford University, the Anglican Church, and Kings College of London University, under the Ancient & Accepted Scottish Rite; the collusion fostered the creation of an occult brotherhood in the Muslim world, dedicated to the use of terrorism on behalf of the Freemasons and Order of the Garter in the City of London. The leading promoters of the Oxford Movement were Prime Minister Benjamin Disraeli, Lord Palmerstone of the Palladian Rite, and Frater Edward Bullwer-Lytton, the leader of a branch of Rosicrucianism that developed from the Asiatic Brethren, or the *Fratres Lucis*. Benjamin Disraeli was Grand Master of Freemasonry, as well as knight of the Order of the Garter.

Bulwer-Lytton was the Grand Patron of the *Societas Rosicruciana in Anglia* (SRIA), founded in 1865 by Frater Robert Wentworth Little, and based on the rituals of Fratres Lucis, had become members of a German Masonic lodge called *L'Aurore Naissante*, or "the Nascent Dawn", founded in Frankfurt-on-Main in 1807. It was at *L'Aurore Naissante* where Lord Bulwer Lytton initiated. In Egypt, the Oxford movement centered on the creation of a "reform" movement of Islam, known as *Salafi*, to serve the Brotherhoods in protecting their trade by the Suez Canal, crucial to the shipment of their oil cargo to Europe and British Colonial India. Jamaluddin al'Afghani enrolled in a madrasah in the holy city of Najaf, in Iraq. There, Afghani initiated into the Babist mysteries of Sheikh ibn Zayn ibn Ibráhím al'Ahsá'í. Ahsá'í was succeeded after his death by Sayyid Kāẓim bin Qāsim al'Husaynī Rashtī, who introduced the idea of a 'perfect Shi'ah,' in Islam called *Bab*, meaning "gate," who is to come.

An initiate of the Babist mysteries, Mírzá Husayn'Alí Núrí, declared himself the emanation of the "One greater than Himself," predicted by the Bab (Sayyid Rashtī), assuming the title of Bahá'u'lláh, Arabic for "Glory of God."   In 1866, Jamaluddin al 'Afghani became confidential counselor to Azam, the Sultan in Afghanistan. In 1871, Afghani went to Cairo, sponsored by Prime Minister Mustafa Pasha, acquainted with him in Istanbul, and then placed him salary, with a prestigious tenure at the university of Al'Azhar. Afghani's theology remained strictly orthodox Shi'a, yet in 1878, he relocated to Cairo's old Jewish quarter, where he announced the formation of the Arab Masonic Society.

Afghani became an initiate of the Hermetic Brotherhood of Luxor in Cairo, Egypt, or the Sabian teachings of the Grand Lodge of the of Cairo Ismāʿīliyya; a fraternal society dedicated to Masonry, philosophy, and Nizari Ismāʿīliyya. In Cairo, Afghani studied with two initiates in the Hermetic Brotherhood of Luxor; James Sanua, and Lydia Pashkov. Sanua and Lydia Pashkov were companions of Helena Petrovna Blavatsky, A Russian mystic who founded the Theosophical Society in 1875. Through her sacred studies and acquaintance with Jamaluddin al'Afghani, Blavatsky assimilated her doctrines of theosophy, derived from Ismāʿīlism, which she would disseminate to the Invisible College of the Western Mystery Schools. Unknown to scholars, Blavatsky cites Afghani anonymously in her tomes, *Isis Unveiled* and *The Secret Doctrine*. She claims to have received these works from a "Persian Sufi", as scholar K. Paul Johnson points out, Afghani is the likely reference.

According to Johnson, a fundamental structure in Blavatsky's theosophy originates from one source; Ismāʿīlism. *The Chaldean Book of Numbers* professes a sevenfold cosmology similar to Nizari Ismāʿīliyya. "The centrality of the number seven", notes Johnson:

" ...is a major clue which points to Ismaili gnosis as an important source for both Blavatsky and Gurdjieff. Henri Corbin's Cyclical Time and Ismaili Gnosis describes the doctrine of a sevenfold cosmic evolutionary process, repeated in a sevenfold historical scheme, paralleled by a sevenfold initiatory path for the individual adept. This corresponds exactly to the Mahatma letters [of Blavatsky] teaching that "the degrees of an Adept's initiation mark the seven stages at which he discovers the secret of the sevenfold principles in nature and man and awakens his dormant powers." The doctrine of the Resurrection acquires a specific meaning in Ismaili gnosis which relates it to Blavatsky's teachings. Each of the seven principles of the individual is "resurrected" by the influence of the next higher principle. HPB's sevenfold breakdown of human principles was presented variously as Chaldean, Tibetan, and Chaldeo-Tibetan. But in fact its closest historical analogue is Ismaili." [The Masters Revealed, pp. 146]

Frater Paschal Beverly Randolph thrust himself into this labyrinth when announcing his intention to publish the secret of the Ansaireh (Nusa'iriyya, a mystical sect of Muslims in Syria known today as the Alawis) priesthood in *The New Mola* (1873). In *Eulis*, he writes of his encounter with a Nusa'iri maiden: "One night - it was in far-off Jerusalem or Bethlehem, I really forget which - I made love to, and was loved by, a dusky maiden of Arabic blood. I of her, and that experience, learned - not directly, but by suggestion - fundamental principle of the White Magic of Love; subsequently I became affiliated with some dervishes and fakirs of whom, by suggestion, still, I found the road to other knowledges; and of these devout practicers of a simple, but sublime and holy magic, I obtained additional clues - little threads of suggestion, which, persistently followed, led my soul into labyrinths of knowledge themselves did not even suspect the existence of. I became practically, what I was naturally - a mystic, and in time chief of the lofty brethren; taking the clues left by the masters, and pursuing them farther than they had ever been before; actually discovering the ELIXIR OF LIFE; the universal Solvent, or celestial Alkahest; the water of beauty and perpetual youth, and the philosopher's stone."

n 1873, Carl Kellner, a fraternal associate of Brother Randolph, was another of the many occultists associated with Egyptian Freemasonry, traveling to Cairo in the time of Afghani's activity. There he met, for the first time, a Luxor initiate by the name of Brother Aya Aziz, also known as Max Théon. Théon was the son of the last leader of the Frankist sect, Rabbi Judes Lion Bimstein of Warsaw, Poland. In Cairo, Théon worked with Blavatsky, and became a student of Paulos Metamon, a Coptic Initiate. Paulos Metamon was

191

also Blavatsky's first tutor, whom she had met in Asia Minor in 1848, and again in Cairo in 1870, as Metamon introduced her to the Hermetic Brotherhood of Light, the Fratres Lucis, and a continuation of the Asiatic Brethren.

Afghani's departed Egypt to Afghanistan, while his pupil, Mohammed Abduh, was inexplicably named the chief editor of the official British colonial press of the Egyptian government, the Journal Official. Working under him was a Freemason, Sa'ad Zaghul, founder of the Wafd nationalist party. Abduh traveled throughout the Arab world, under various names, particularly to Tunis, Beirut, and Damascus, Syria. In each city he journeyed, Abduh initiated members into the secret society of Afghani's Salafi fundamentalism. The secret Salafi movement then became allied with the Wahhabis of Saudi Arabia, through the doctrines of another Arab Freemason, Mohammed Rashid Rida. After the death of Afghani in 1897, and Abduh in 1905, Rida assumed the leadership of the Salafi secret society.

The Society of the Muslim Brothers chartered in 1928 in Cairo, Egypt by the Islamic scholar and schoolteacher Sheikh Hasan Ahmed Abdel Rahman Muhammed al'Banna. When Hasan al'Banna was twelve years old, he became a student of the *Hasafiya Sufi order*, becoming a fully initiated member in 1922. Banna's father was as student of Abduh, and himself was greatly influenced by Rashid Rida's Salafi fundamentalism. The Muslim Brotherhood originated as a religious social organization, tutoring the illiterate, establishing charitable hospitals and providing endowment for local enterprises. As the Brotherhood's social influence widened starting in 1936, it began to stridently oppose British colonialism in Egypt.

In 1952 the Egyptian monarch King Farouk I was overthrown by nationalist military officers led by Colonel Gamel Abdel Nasser and General Muhammad Naguib supported by the Brotherhood. On 26 October, an assassination attempt was carried out against Nasser during a rally in Alexandria. The attempt to assassinate Nasser was suspected by the Brotherhood. This led to the regime acting against the Brotherhood, executing Brotherhood leaders on 9 December in 1954. The Brotherhood was banned and this time thousands of its members were imprisoned, many of them held for years in prisons and concentration camps, and tortured. On February 12, 1949 in Cairo, al'Banna who was a Freemason, was assassinated.

The influence of Freemasonry in Egypt and Arab countries struggling with post-colonial revolutionary sentiment cannot be overlooked. Hanna Abi Rashid, chief of the masonic lodge in Beirut, wrote: *"Jamaluddin al'Afghani was the chief of the masonic lodge in Egypt, which had about three hundred members, most of whom were scholars and state officials. After him, the leading master Muhammad 'Abduh became the chief. 'Abduh was a leading freemason. No one can deny that he has spread the masonic spirit in Arab countries."* [Da'irat al'maarif al'masoniyya, p. 197, Beirut, 1381/1961.] *"As revealed by Abduh, al'Afghani developed in his students a practical inclination: he encouraged them to engage in the publication of magazines, to put in motion a current of opinion and to join, like he himself did, the masonic lodges of French inspiration."* (Tariq Ramadan, Aux Sources du Renouveau musulman, D'al-Alfghani a Hassan al'Banna un siecle de reformisme islamique, Paris: 1998, p. 54)

"At the same time Afghani started to introduce himself into the French circles of freemasonry. He introduced, as we have seen, the Egyptian intellectuals of his entourage who were to be, later, the principal actors of the 'Urabi Revolution. These circles had a crucial importance for al-Afghani: not only because they allowed him to spread his ideas but also because he was able to meet with influential people in the political environment. Thus we can affirm,

without any doubt, that this is the period, in which al'Afghani, thanks to the recognition and to the personal engagement in the creation of an associative body conceived on the model of the masonic circles, was able to accentuate his involvement in establishing political influence and alliance with the powers." (ibid., p. 85)

"*In this period Afghani came forward as a political figure in two ways: by using a Freemasonic lodge as a vehicle for political intrigue and change, and by influencing people through oratory.*" (Ali Rahnema, Pioneers of Islamic Revival, London: 1979, p. 17) "*The Documents corroborate and help to date Afghani's membership and activity in the freemasons of Egypt....Most discussions of Afghani's masonic activity begin it in 1877 or 1878, but the Documents include a letter from him applying for membership in a masonic lodge which dates from the spring of 1875 and a note saying he had entered a lodge in Muharram 1293/February 1876. Unfortunately the name or rite of the lodge is not included. The Documents also include invitations to sessions of Italian lodges from early 1877 through 1879 and documents beginning in January 1877, from the Eastern Star Lodge, which was affiliated with the Grand Lodge of England....The lodge, with al'Afghani as its leader, was to become an important instrument in the growing Egyptian crisis of 1878 and 1879.*" (Nikki R. Keddie, Sayyid Jamaluddin al'Afghani," Berkeley: 1972, p. 92)

After the attempted assassination of Nasser in 1954, the Egyptian government used the incident to justify political oppression of the Muslim Brotherhood, imprisoning a young Sayyid Qutb and many members for their vocal opposition to the Nasser regime. Sayyid Qutb was prolific author, tutor, Islamic theologian, poet, and leading scholar of the Egyptian Muslim Brotherhood in the 1950s and '60s. Qutb died during his imprisonment by Nasser's suppression in 1966.

Mohammed Qutb, Sayyid's brother, along with other prisoners in the Muslim Brotherhood, took political refuge under CIA sponsorship in Saudi Arabia following Nasser's crackdown. He was given different official positions at Saudi universities to teach and to carry out the mission of the Muslim Brotherhood. While in Saudi Arabia, Mohammed Qutb conceived of the organization now known as the World Assembly of Muslim Youth (WAMY), which was established in 1972, thanks to large donations from the wealthy Saudi bin Laden family.

Sayyid Qutb synchronized the core theological doctinres of modern Islamic theology: the Kharijites' *takfir*, ibn Taymiyya's fatwas and social prescriptions, Rashid Rida's salafism, Maududi's concept of the contemporary *jahiliyya* and Hassan al'Banna's political activism. Mohammed Qutb taught at Mecca's Umm al'Qura University, and King Abdul'aziz University in Jeddah. One of his fellow students was an aspiring Egyptian doctor, Ayman al 'Zawahiri. He eventually became one of Egyptian Islamic Jihad's strategic managers and recruiter. While attending King Abdul Aziz University in Jeddah, Osama bin Laden also became acquainted with Mohammed Qutb, and initiated into the Muslim Brotherhood. In 1979, Bin Laden left Saudi Arabia, being one of the first Arabs to join mujahedeen fighting against Soviet invasion in Afghanistan. Osama Bin Laden, at just twenty-two years of age, established the MAK, the *Maktab al'Khidamat*, or the Mujahedeen Services Bureau, based in Peshawar, Pakistan. George Bush Sr., as vice president under President Ronald Reagan, was in charge of the covert operations that supported the MAK. The MAK was nurtured by Pakistan's ISI, Inter-Services Intelligence, and linked up with Pakistan's Muslim Brotherhood organization, the *Jamaat-e Islami*, founded by Abul Ala Maududi, to recruit mujahedeen in Afghanistan.

By the late 1980s, the *Maktab al'Khidamat* expanded in fifty countries around the world. Osama bin Laden then recognized that prospective Mujahedeen of the *Maktab al'Khidamat* did not have any military or intelligence training, and established the *Bayt al'Ansar* in Peshawar, Pakistan as a central training base, or *al 'Qaeda*. Sufis are the link in the Invisible College that has made Islam the world's second-largest and fastest growing religion, with 1.2 billion adherents. Not a sect of Islam, Sufis are heirs of a nameless faith, hidden within both the Sunni and Shia branches of Islam, Sufis have through the centuries combined their secrets with the defense and expansion of Islamic mysticism. At once mystics and elite soldiers, dervishes and preachers, philanthropists and social workers, Sufis have always been in the vanguard of the Invisible College.

Without understanding the esoteric roots of the Sufis, we cannot understand the origins of contemporary political undercurrents in the Middle East. For radical fundamentalists like the Saudi Wahhabiyya and the Taliban, the Sufis are deadly enemies, who draw on mystical practices alien to the Quran. Where fundamentalist Muslims like Ayatollah Ruhollah Khomeini, and secular Baathist dictators like Saddam Hussein, Bashar al 'Assad, and Muammar Gadhafi rose to power, Sufis were persecuted and driven underground. For many mainstream Muslims and Muslimahs, Sufism is simply part of the air they breathe. Engineering global peace is not contingent on a decline or secularization of Islam, but a renewal and strengthening of the antique faith, safeguarded by evanescent Sufis.

No longer is there such a thing as *"occult."* The Internet casts a dull digital ruddiness on rituals, ciphers, and initiation ceremonies once kept in repositories of sacred silence by the Invisible College and it's custodians of the nameless faith. Sufi mystics are prodigies having charted a new expanse across the mind, body, and soul to the farthest reaches of consciousness and space-time continuum. They are part of an elite heritage with pedigreed secrets and an unbroken current of antique faith. American Occultism and the spurious groups that populate it, do not, and never have, fully grasped the contributions of Sufis to the spiritual and psychological enhancement of the human species. Occult organizations such as the Golden Dawn, Thelemic orders, Satanic groups, Freemasons, and Rosy Cross societies profess to initiate men (and women) into the mysteries, and foster spiritual development. These groups do not extend the fraternal grip of interfaith dialogue and cultural inclusion in their rosters.

Sufis and Muslims in American esoteric orders such as the Hermetic Order of the Golden Dawn®, and the Ordo Templi Orientis®, account for less than 5% of Membership rosters. I inquired of the late Dr. Christopher S. Hyatt about the ethnic membership demographics of various American occult orders. Dr. Hyatt was the student and life-long friend of Israel Regardie, a prolific writer on esoteric studies, Rosicrucianism, student of Aleister Crowley, and Adept of the Golden Dawn tradition. Dr. Hyatt was involved in the resuscitation of numerous Golden Dawn lineages and groups, he was acquainted with members of over a dozen American occult organizations, and held high level degrees in several, including Ordo Templi Orientis®. My inquiries seemed to have struck a chord with Dr. Hyatt who advised me professionally and spiritually intermittently from 2005 to 2007.

Dr. Hyatt stated that during his tenure with Ordo Templi Orientis®, and his administration of the Thelemic Order of the Golden Dawn from 1990 to 1994, and the Hermetic Society and Temple of the Golden Dawn in the early 1990s that *Muslims and non-whites were discouraged from joining these organizations*. The few Muslims who applied for membership in these groups received no response or had their petitions denied. Muslims and non-whites, such as African-Americans, Latinos, Asians, and Native Americans accounted for less than 5% of membership in American Occult organizations. Since the majority of these "magical societies" do not produce membership demographics to the public due to the exclusive nature of spiritual teachings, critics to this volume could agree the factual basis and degrees of ethnic racism and marginalization.

We challenge any American occult organization to publicly produce membership registers proving otherwise.

Thelemic philosopher and occultist Aleister Crowley voiced a disdain for Islam, Judaism, and Christianity while collecting and choosing mystic teachings in each of these three religions that suited his occult aspirations. The affirmation of belief in a supreme being is of no special consequence in Thelema. Crowley insists: "whether you are a Christian or a Buddhist, a Theist, an Atheist, or Pagan; the attainment of this one state of mystical realization is as open to you as is nightmare, or madness, or intoxication." (The Gospel According to Saint Bernard Shaw, p. 117) In the Holy Books of Thelema, Crowley instructs the Neophyte that "To the adept, seeing all these things from above, there seems nothing to choose between Buddha and Mohammed, between Atheism and Theism." (Liber X, v. 19) Liber LXV even praises and blesses the "parricidal pomp of atheists" beheld by the speaker in its fifth chapter (vv. 34-37). Crowley continues, "The God-idea must go with other relics of the Fear born of Ignorance into the limbo of savagery." (The Law Is for All, p. 112) Crowley and his adherents believed Islam a mere nonsense suited to the intelligence of the peoples among whom it was promulgated. Thelemic philosophy espoused by Crowley aligned with divergent premises of atheism and polytheism in Thelema are incoherent, but Crowley insists

198

that this outcome is a natural function of the incoherence in the vulgar conception of God. Crowley and Thelemites clearly lack any spiritual maturity in discerning the value of religion and the mystic traditions derived from them such as Sufism, while fostering such practices like the "Gnostic Mass," and "Ecclesia Gnostica Catholica." American occultism exists as an axis between radical conservative political extremists and neo-Nazi enterprises including David Griffin's *Hermetic Order of the Golden Dawn / Rosicrucian A+O®*, Robert Zink's *Esoteric Order of the Golden Dawn*, David Myatt's *Order of Nine Angels*, and Charles Cicero's Hermetic Order of the Golden Dawn, Inc.® Myatt and Griffin each have organizational ties to white supremacist movements in Great Britain, and Canada.

Rosicrucian Fraternities active in the United States include *Antiquus Mysticusque Ordo Rosæ Crucis* (AMORC) governed by Imperator Christian Bernard, Confraternity of the Rose Cross under Imperator Gary L. Stewart, Societas Rosicruciana in Civitatibus Foederatis under "Supreme Magi" William H. Koon II, and Fraternitas Rosicruciana Antiqua under Parsival Krumm-Heller all currently are operated by Anglo-Saxon Caucasian males.

Every active Golden Dawn organization currently initiating prospects has been administered historically by Anglo-Saxon Caucasian males. Contemporary neo-Satanic organizations, many of which project aversion to the Masonic Mystical Christian paradigm, espouse sexual equality for women have had Anglo-Saxon Caucasian males operate their organizations. I include David Myatt's Order of Nine Angels, Dr. Michael Aquino's Temple of Set, and Peter Gilmore's Church of Satan in this axis of radical conservative extremists and neo-Nazi enterprises.

Soror Laailah and I operated the Ordo Antichristianus Illuminati® in 2003 synchronizing Tantric practice, experimental psychology, expressionist art, music theory, and social activism with occultism. I initiated into the O∴A∴I∴ in 1999 when it operated as a Luciferian guild under Dr. Christopher S. Hyatt's occult students. On September 11, 2001 I began directing the O∴A∴I∴ in the office of Cancellarius. Soror Laailah and I reconstituted the organization in 2003, overseeing all administrative duties. Shortly in the months before we assumed complete responsibility and duties for the direction of this esoteric current, the O∴A∴I∴ received an influx of petitions and inquiries from a small number of Muslims, Freemasons, and Thelemites. Many of the prospects who initiated during this time in the summer of 2003 presently remain our dearest friends and most valued Fratres and Sorores.

As membership in the O∴A∴I∴ increased, different persons from all spiritual backgrounds initiated; Freemasons, luciferians, artists, wiccans, Rosicrucians, and even Sufi Muslims. One practicing Muslim, who was a student at U.S.C. (University of Southern California) at the time, petitioned for membership in the O∴A∴I∴. Basem learned of the O∴A∴I∴ through a mutual friend of his, a thelemite who initiated earlier. He took the motto *Frater El Ras El Ghul* and informed me he had family in Egypt that would be willing to assist us in touring Egypt.

When I returned from Canada in 2004, Basem had put me in contact with his family in Egypt. Frater Basem's cousins, Ayman and Amany, were attending college in USC and graduating the same year. While on holiday, Ayman and Amany agreed to assist with lodging and travel around Cairo, Egypt. I traveled to Egypt and assembled with my mentors in Berlin, Germany before traveling to Cairo. Amany introduced me to Sufi mysticism, as we began a lifelong correspondence and friendship. Amany and her cousins share a wealthy affluent family high on Egyptian social strata. At midnight before the vernal equinox, I knelt in the desert before my German mentor, Frau Erica, and Amany.

It was about two hours before midnight local Cairo time. Our party met with Boutrour and two other individuals dressed in business casual at the Giza site entrance grounds. Amany spoke at length in Arabic to Boutrour and the two gentlemen. Frau Erica and Frater Eckhart had a brief discussion with Boutrour and his colleagues. Amany stared into me looking but without eyes ... a transference of souls... body within body ... holding where lost souls go. Lights were on the Pyramids and Amany's face. I could see makeshift pavilions set up, with sofas, chairs, and other loungers. Dimly lit lamps dotted the area around the Pyramids. A line of armed guards stretched out in front of the entrance a few hundred yards behind, I could see at least a hundred, likely more, lines of silhouettes walking about the pyramids and down near the sphinx. Boutrour's discussion with Frau Erica and Frater ended.

What I witnessed after midnight by the Great Pyramids of Gizeh would rival American Hollywood imagination. Attendees of the "Bohemian Grove-esque" venue were European entertainment celebrities, Americans, yet primarily Arab financiers, and statesmen. Arabic and Greek chanting acted as a stimulant and precursor to ritual group sex and bacchanalia, culminating in the most intense, erotic, and depraved sexual activity. Afterward the drugs wore down, bodies were removed. Senators, Musicians, Ministers, artists, scientists, poets ... the Elite all went back to their resorts & palaces. And the world remained as it was. Unaware. Yes..it is the way it's been done. Within the walls of the Vatican, inside New York City and Las Vegas mansions, inside the Louvre at night, inside the Berlin Museum, inside Palaces, Libraries, Museums, Legislative buildings, Grand Lodges, and inside the sanctuaries of Grand Priories. Exotic elegance in erotic convergence.

A week after my initiations at the Great Pyramids and the ritual events, I was meeting Amany every evening for tea along with her friends and family. I learned of their involvement in Sufi *tariqas* and the rich history of Sufism and its development in Egypt and encompassing all Islamic culture. Their knowledge of Sufism was esoteric and exclusive. During my research I learned that Amany had experienced similar initiations under different cultural context. One evening over tea, Amany and I were sitting in a local café enjoying a sheesha. She invited me to meet her older sister visiting from Alexandria in a few days. I had already met her younger sister, Nouni and looked forward to being introduced to more of this enigmatic woman's family.

While Amany possessed striking classic beauty, and her sister Nouni was very young, shy and attractive, her older sister Basma was stunning and beautiful. Like Amany she exhibited an air of unchallenged confidence. Basma, Amany, her cousins and I sat and chatted at Amany's apartment in Cairo. Her cousins retired later in the evening leaving Amany, Basma, and I chatting some more. Basma inquired about my reasons for initiating inside the Great Pyramid, and participating in the group ritual later at midnight. Basma, like my mentor Frau Erica who with her mate Frater Eckhart returned to Berlin earlier in the week, shared knowledge about a Cabal of contiguous secret societies operating as custodians of advanced knowledge embedded in the human genotype.

The Cabal is an archaic confederation with some of its delegates well place in the strategic echelons of social strata. It has spawned varied occult guilds and esoteric movements for over a thousand years. Artisans and initiates in the Cabal have shaped music, literature, our ideas of romanticism, theatre, the study of the mind, and scientific advancements. There is no legitimate occult society in America or Europe operating at present that has not derived from the Cabal. Many derivatives and their affiliate orders, of the Christian fraternal societies such as the Gregorian and Benedictine orders, the Fratres Crucigeri cum Rubea Stella, the Cathari, and Rosy Cross societies would argue vehemently over their alleged connections or absence of, to the 'black rose,' or Black Chapel Cabal.

The Cabal cascades into every modern fraternal organization, every political and economic stratum, and every global corporate network. The Cabal offers the sincere student of the Mysteries a long and distinguished pedigree for over a thousand years. Re-emerging from the social and political turmoil of the medieval atmosphere plagued by Roman Catholic pestilence, the "black rose" societies were chartered contiguously. The originating tales of many of the same groups are intentionally vague, elusive in poorly kept, or non-extant records or oral narrative. The ideal is the perseverance of secrecy and critical information. A Cabal such as the 'black rose,' or by any name it is referred to in the 21st century, if at all, descends from Mystery Cults predating Christendom in the Roman Imperium.

The three of us continued chatting about the esoteric histories of the Cabal, while I shared with them the involvement of many of my family members in Freemasonry, the Order of the Eastern Star, and other fraternal societies. I brought up my family a lot in the conversation and the working knowledge I had of our heritage. Basma offered to introduce me "*to some of my sisters I think you'd be interested in meeting, maybe they can help you with your research ay?*" Basma, Amany, and their uncle Boutrour accompanied me shortly before I was scheduled to return home to America in early April, to a beautiful Egyptian mosque in the Cairo metro area. Basma was wearing an elegant gold and white hijab. Amany was wearing a casual yellow hijab with a green and yellow dress that accented her attractiveness.

We entered the mosque a few hours after evening prayer, the interior beauty adorned with art was incredible and scaled to about the size of at least 3 large Roman Catholic cathedrals. This was a dream I was reliving from a lost memory in my consciousness. Walking through the halls and rooms automatically thrust me into a state of walking meditation and theta-wave conscious activity. We entered a large room with two younger men conversing with an older Sheikh dressed in white. Boutrour introduced me as I bowed cordially to the Sheikh. He and Basma alternated in conversing with the Sheikh in Arabic. Amany translated quietly; Basma was making some sort of petition on behalf of myself to meet with older female Muslimahs at another location near the Mosque. For some reason unknown to me, we had to petition the Sheikh for this meeting. The Sheikh asked my name, where I was from, and what school I attended in the United States.

Sheikh ended his conversation with Boutrour and Basma, and addressed his two assistants briefly. Sheikh's two assistants escorted us outside the mosque and led us in their vehicle to a large house about twenty-minutes driving distance away. Boutrour and our party followed behind in his car. The manor we arrived at thirty minutes later was gated and had two gentleman with sidearms waiting for us outside. The two assistants to the Sheikh parked outside and exited their vehicle. We exited Boutrour's vehicle, and to my interest the two armed gentleman seemed familiar with Basma and deferred to her. Basma led me up a small footpath up to the door. *"When is your flight back to the states again?"* *"April 21"* I answered. *"Ah, good, what airlines are you taking?"* I said *"KLM Royal Dutch to Amsterdam then JFK,"* while we waited as someone inside answered the door. A young woman in her 20s answered the door for Basma and motioned us inside, glancing at me suspiciously.

Basma and Amany greeted a stunningly gorgeous Arabic woman on a sofa sipping some tea using a computer. I later learned she was also Egyptian. The woman I guessed in her early thirties bounced up and hugged Basma and Amany as if long lost sisters. Amany introduced me in Arabic as the three of them conversed at length. I stood there, the awkward nerdish American, a pilgrim from an unholy land. I felt as if I was observing a reunion between life-long friends or family members. *"Eh another American, where are you from Joshua?"* The commotion alerted others in the manor because five other striking women appeared in the hallway coming into the parlour we were seated in. Another American? How many Americans interested in secret societies had they been acquainted with? *"I live in Arizona."* I replied, while Amany and Basma greeted and embraced the five other women warmly.

The five new women were just as captivating and gorgeous as Basma and the woman who initially greeted us. They all wore casual Islamic attire yet as the dirty American; I could not help but notice their curves. Introductions were made with Basma introducing me to each of the women in Arabic then each to me in English. I learned they were all from different ethnic backgrounds: the woman who initially greeted us was related to Egyptian former King H.M. Fu'ad II, two were Jordanian royalty 28 and 30 years old respectively, and the remaining three were Saudi royalty, ages 31, 33, and 36 respectively. One of the Saudi women appeared to be the representative of the group. Keeping silent the majority of the time, she peered at me in a way that left me extremely unsettled.

The conversation quickly turned from introductions to my explanation of visiting Egypt and initiating at the Great Pyramids, and participating in the group sacraments later at midnight. Basma often interjected to converse and translate with them in Arabic as I explained myself at their behest. The women were interested in discussing my family heritage, my personal spirituality, political ideologies, and experience with secret societies. Surprisingly, the women were aware of what Freemasonry was. The discussion turned to Islam and Sufism. These women were Muslimahs in their public and professional lives, but belonged to a Cabal whose existence is only hinted about in various pieces of new world order conspiracies, and the "September 11 truth movements." As the discussions progressed, I began to feel increasingly uncomfortable; nonetheless, my inquisitiveness could not rest.

The women were part of an antique faith, true sisters initiated higher in esoteric understanding of magick and metaphysics within the secret degrees of the Invisible College than any American. They explained that Sufism was a grand demarcation between Islam and religion; an exterior college of our antique and nameless faith. Where American occultism is concerned with the pursuit and collection of hidden teachings and the engineering of consciousness, Sufism's concern is for scientific progress, social justice and equality, artistic expression, and psychological health. The women spoke of divine intoxication, love, and human suffering. The Cabal they spoke of and represented, along with my mentor Frau Erica, and later I learned, Sister Basma, is the biography of our species.

The Roman Society of Dionysius, Ritual erotica, or sex magic and rites of thaumaturgy was introduced into Rome (c. 200BC) from the Greek culture of lower Italia through Greek-influenced Etruria. Bacchanalia as the mystery society was called, were held in secret, and attended by women only, on three days in the year in the grove of Simila near the Aventine Hill, on March 16 and 17. The bull, the serpent, the ivy, and wine were symbols of Bacchanalian rites, infused with the unquenchable life of the deity. Secret admissions to the rites were extended to men and celebrations took place five times a month.

The Bacchantes remained a considerable society hidden behind developments and prodigious minds in art, music, literature, theatre, and erotica. The Cabal charted new courses in the arts and remained secret under various secret societies, never appearing under the same name - always under a different name or occupation, uncovering new modes of sexual expression and erotica within world religions, their scriptures, and occult organizations. They already have revolutionized culture, leading new approaches to technology and social development; pioneering explorations in psychology and technology that will synthesize information with matter. My Arabic hosts detailed to me, the 'Cabal' known by its many monikers and presented in Islamic culture some of the most intricate and detailed rites of sex magick in Ibn al'Farid's *Ta'iyyatu'l-kubra*, Shahab al'Din Suhrawardi's *Hayakil al-nur* (*The Temples of Light*), Suhrawardi's *Aql-i Surkh* (*The Red Intellect*) and his *Fi Haqiqat al'Ishaq* (On the reality of love), Farīduddīn Attār's *Mokhtar-Nama*, and *The Perfumed Garden of Sensual Delight* (Arabic: روض العاطر في لا نزهة الخاطر *Al'rawd Al'âtir fi Nuzhat Al'khâtir*) by Muhammad al'Nafzawi.

The women representing this Cabal disclosed that Sufism was the parent of Freemasonry and various American occult traditions that have since erred from their Eastern origins. For the next few hours my striking hosts discussed the synchronicity of Islamic secret societies, and the development of organizations such as the Wahhabiyya, and Muslim Brotherhood. Each of the women took turns in the discussion. They interjected each other when necessary, piecing together the synchronicity of Islamic mystical orders like *Roshaniyya* of Pir Roshan, *al'Anṣāriyyah* centred in Syria, the *Aïssâwiyya* centred in Morocco, and the *Jama'at al-Hashishiyya* founded by Hassan Ibn Sabbāh which Basma and I already had discussed at great length.

These four occult schools functioned as the operative roots of Islamic mysticism and American occult traditions. Syncretism is the closely guarded secret of these mystic

207

Islamic schools. The combination of various mystical systems into one coherent culture of illumination has always been the cornerstone of the Cabal's teachings in the Invisible College, of which American occult groups like the Golden Dawn and Rosy Cross are merely lower manifestations of. American occultism had co-opted the teachings and used it within the past hundred years to enslave European society. Since American occultism contains irrevocable European roots, American occult organizations are the most insidious form of social distortion and corruption. American and European secret societies had corrupted our antique faith's syncretic teachings, the evanescent Art of the Cabal.

Our discussion shifted to modern organizations I was familiar with, as I explained my family's involvement in Freemasonry, the Order of the Eastern Star, and other fraternal organizations. I discussed with the two Jordanian women my involvement in American "occult organizations" like the Golden Dawn that piqued the discussion and attention of the entire group. One of the older Saudi women who had been mostly silent up to this point in the discussion, turned the subject of Masonic involvement in American politics (we were discussing which recent US Presidents were Freemasons, and the affiliation of the Bush family with the Skull and Bones Society) to the September 11 attacks. *"So who do you feel is responsible?"* the Saudi woman intoned. *"It doesn't matter; there are a lot of conspiracies about it being an 'inside job,' but who knows."* I replied. *"No no, it does matter,"* she intoned louder, *"people will rise up, protesting what is given to them freely, the attacks were against us...against our faith...our culture. For the secretive groups like Skull and Bones to separate knowledge and joining cultures from the people. Who runs your military? American soldiers have bases all over the middle east, in Afghanistan, Saudi Arabia, Kuwait, Qatar, Turkey, now Iraq...these are holy places...where our antique faith began.*

Not just Islam but enlightened teaching that all European philosophers in your occult traditions sought. It was Sufis who taught your Rosy Christians and first Freemasons!"

The Saudi royal sister was right. The Muslim Brotherhood was founded by a Freemason, Sheikh Hasan al'Banna. The *Bayt al'Ansar* or *al 'Qaeda* was established by American counter-intelligence CIA incentives under the direction of President Bush. The founders of *al 'Qaeda*, Osama Bin Laden, and Abdullah Yusuf Azzam operated under American counter-intelligence liaisons. Cadres of statesmen, financial executives of major global financial institutions like the Financial Stability Board, International Monetary Fund, and Bank for International Settlements, and European consuls assumed total control of all fraternal societies in the European Union and United States.

Sectarianism sold out the syncretism of the antique faith that was parented by Arabian Magi and Sufi theologians centuries before the charters of the first Free Mason lodges. The Masonic lodges and Rosicrucian Societies that parented the Golden Dawn arguably influenced Ordo Templi Orientis®, Thelemic and Luciferian groups were all administered by Anglo-Saxon Caucasian males with ties to militant political anarchist cadres. The Islamic terrorists that carried out the September 11 attacks, the very same mujahedeen that waged guerilla warfare against Soviet invasion during the 1980s, were bankrolled by the Central Intelligence Agency, and the Bank of Credit and Commerce International founded by Pakistani financier Agha Hasan Abedi, himself a Freemason and occultist.

BCCI launched an international monopolies with its purchase in 1976 of 85% of the Banque de Commerce et Placements (BCP) of Geneva, Switzerland. After the BCCI liquidated this bank it installed Alfred Hartmann as chief executive. Hartmann then became the chief financial officer for BCC Holding and was affiliated with the Rothschild family, sitting on the the board of directors of N.M. Rothschild & Sons, London, and president of Rothschild Bank AG of Zurich. BCCI was initially incorporated in Luxembourg, famous for its lax banking restrictions, and soon branches and holding companies sprouted up around the globe: in the Cayman Islands, the Netherlands Antilles, Hong Kong, Abu Dhabi, and Washington DC. BCCI's main route of investment was financing Israeli arms into Afghanistan during the Soviet invasion. The majority of this information was discussed among my five Arabian hosts, Amany, Basma, and I.

The intermediate cadres, the Knights of Malta, Ancient and Accepted Scottish Rite of Freemasonry, Order of the Eastern Star, York Rite of Freemasonry, Ordine Militare e Religioso dei Cavalieri di Cristo, Benevolent and Protective Order of Elks, and Golden Dawn organizations once contributed service and endowment to humanity, and hold the family as sacred. Presently, organizations like O.T.O., Golden Dawn and its derivatives, even Masonic Rites and appendent bodies operate and recruit under false pretenses of initiation. These "esoteric" cadres attach to themselves the brand of "magical orders," and "occultism' under the pretense of empowerment and equality. There is no cultural diversity and equality in these cadres. There is no ethnic inclusion other than Anglo-Saxon and Caucasians, all under the direction of males. There are no Native Americans, African-Americans, Asians, or Arabs and Muslims in the higher tiers of their initiation degrees.

During this discussion with our hosts, it occurred to me, that indictments of prejudice and political militancy in American and European occult cadres was certainly hypocritical coming from Arabs who represented their own secretive mystical brotherhoods. I took this position up with Basma and our hosts: *"That's not fair, how many mystic Islamic sects include Americans and Europeans? How many*

210

Sufi tariqas accept non-Muslims, and people who aren't Arabs or speak Arabic?" "Most of them," the older Saudi women countered, *"Sufi tariqas are active in Indonesia, Malaysia, India, even Canada, and in the States. All over the globe, and we accept you regardless of your race. We don't care about your race, if you want to study schools in the antique faith you study with Sufis. Do Buddhists exclude people because of ethnicity or race? There are a lot of Buddhist monks who are not Tibetan or Asian."* My counter was over before it started. *"Oh."* Was all I could manage. They were right. Zen Buddhists, Sufis, Native American shamanism, Santeria, and Voudou - all these traditions actively accepted and recruited individuals from all ethnicities. American and European "occult" cadres did not.

We were our own enemy. The September 11 attacks were not self-inflicted foreign policy failures, nor the violent jihad of a global terrorist network; the war is a culmination of a shadow war between the remnants of the Cabal's antique faith, and European-American cadres of secret societies that co-opted and abused the Invisible College for its own selfish political power. Disinformation reigns supreme in the age of the Internet, Facebook, and YouTube. We challenge our readers to go out and talk to people, disconnect and reconnect.

I did not wish to discuss secret societies, politics, or religion and social justice with mystical women anymore. I wanted to return home, watch classic films and pretend this world did not exist. Frau Erica was right about my initiations at the Pyramids, the schools of our antique faith are the pillars of social progress; there influence in social strata is not linear; it is recursive and exponential. New social strata will replace obsolete social strata as painlessly as nature will allow. Writing a history of the Cabals enshrouds the knowledge of secret influences behind great events. Our technologies and paramedia break down reality tunneling of

211

the past; secret societies are becoming replaced by Media Mystery Schools. Too much information has been released.

Amany and I finished the shisha in another large parlour where our discussions had moved. The hosts arose from their computers and shishas which they had attended too diligently while taking turns in the conversation, and retired to other rooms. Each of them made eye contact as they left, speaking with Basma and Amany briefly before they left, holding their gaze at me long enough to let me know I was not to reveal their identities. The older Saudi woman was the last to leave and reiterated Basma's instructions to me in English never to reveal the identities of the hosts, nor the details of what occurred nearly a week ago during the group sacraments at the Great Pyramids, or who was present. Basma later informed me that unknown to me, she and the older Saudi woman were present during the group rite that lasted several hours outside the Pyramids.

"*People will rise up and die in the protesting.*" Basma said while the older Saudi spoke to Amany quietly in Arabic. "*Our generation is revolutionary, we're creating a cultural conversion to a global community.*" Social media, and entrepreneurial global networks will enact revolutionary changes in social strata and technology that will rupture the fabric of human emotion and artistic expression. The schools of the antique faith were custodians centuries before the formation of the first Christian monastic orders, the first charters of Masonic lodges, and the Templars; The Invisible Colleges of the East were pillars of art, classics, literature, music, spiritual fraternity, and the sciences . They were a Cabal of imperious love and artistic understanding of the darkest depths of the human condition.

Basma and the Arabian "Sufi" women were precise. Within years, the American economy, teetered on the brink of collapse causing a global depressive conditions in GDP, unemployment, consumer spending, and credit circulation.

The United States' first African-American was elected President, an inspiring event regardless of political policies he labored to enact, and failed to enact. A malicious and vitriolic campaign followed a national debate on universal health care coverage and the age-old philosophic argument of government involvement in the private sector of American consumers and working class. Discontent grew with a generation fed up with oligarchy and ruinous economic disparity. Protests and demonstrations began in Egypt in 2007, intensifying in 2009 and 2010 to include violent demonstrations against oligarchic corruption in Tunisia and Egypt, and Theocratic rule in Iran.

The Mubarak regime in Egypt was swiftly overthrown by young revolutionaries in Tahrir Square that inspired an entire global community. Violent war and civil strife engulfed Libya and Syria, with mass demonstrations spreading through Yemen and Algeria. Riots broke out in Greece and Great Britain against austerity measures in the Eurozone debt crisis. Thousands began protesting in the United States against Wall Street, protests and demonstrations against economic disparity that grew to a global scale. All inspired by Egyptian revolutionaries.

The schools of the antique faith long have been the custodians of renaissance in art, music, the sciences, and humanities. The fraternal institutions which labor to co-opt centuries after centuries of evolution and spirituality embedded in the genome continue their occult teachings of sectarianism under false pretense. The first shot in a global occult war was fired a decade ago. Since the September 11 attacks, America has befallen to ill catastrophes: the Space Shuttle Columbia disaster, Hurricanes Katrina and Rita, Economic depression, and war in Iraq (which began on the Vernal Equinox of 2003, a time when Mars had been closest to Earth not since millennia) costing billions. We are our own enemy. Basma and my Arabic sisters were precise years ago. The Intifada had already begun. The generals of the stones were ready.

L

www.ingramcontent.com/pod-product-compliance
Lightning Source LLC
Chambersburg PA
CBHW031547260326

41914CB00002B/302